Mechanix ILLUSTRATED
How-To-Do-It
Encyclopedia

Edited by the Combined Staffs of
MECHANIX ILLUSTRATED and FAWCETT BOOKS

IN TWENTY VOLUMES

VOLUME 3

COMPLETE CONTENTS AND INDEX IN VOLUME 20

Ba-Bo

THE DANBURY PRESS

It costs less if you can find space for an added bathroom within the present structure of your house. The next best arrangement to add space is to enclose all or part of a porch, as is being done here, above.

NOW YOU CAN . . .

add a bathroom

IF YOU CAN FIND a place for added bathroom facilities without building an addition to your house, the cost will be far less. If you can't find space within the existing structure, perhaps you can enclose all or part of a porch.

If there is no other choice, and you have to build an addition to gain the space needed, keep in mind that the room you add need not be the bathroom. It may work out better in your house plan to add a new bathroom, or some other room, and convert some part of your existing space to the bathroom. Here's why: The closer you are to existing pipes, the lower will be your costs. Further, the closer you are to existing plumbing, the easier it will be to hide pipes.

Where to Put a Bath. You can squeeze a full bath in a space as small as 54x78 inches. You can often get this much space by removing the wall in back-to-back closets. The untraveled end of a hall may

have 30 or more square feet, and if it does, it can serve. You may be able to find the space under a stairway, or under the eaves in an attic. If the headroom is low, you may have to dispense with a shower, but you can still have a tub.

You can convert a pantry or a laundry. In the pantry, you still may be able to preserve much of the storage space by means of a storage wall. In converting a laundry, by use of modern appliances, there still may be space for clothes washing. You can either get a combination washer-dryer, or stack the dryer over the washer.

You can divide an existing large bath into two bathrooms, or at least into 1½ baths. Since the tub is the least used of the three fixtures, it could be shared between the two new rooms.

A half bath (lavatory and toilet) requires only 30x60 inches. You can fit one into a walk-in closet. A toilet and shower can be accommodated in a 3-foot wide slice

Use a skylight to bring natural daylight to an inside bathroom. Drop the level of the ceiling down to accommodate pipes overhead. A new ceiling of acoustical tile is quick, easy to install.

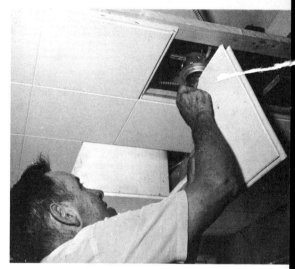

Every bathroom needs one or more ventilators to expel vapor, odors, and bring in fresh air. A squirrel-cage type is best for handling large quantities of air quickly, with minimum sound.

Lowering ceiling makes bathroom cozier, easier to heat. Acoustical tiles will provide both sound and thermal insulation. Tile, at right, is being marked for cut around NuTone heater unit outlet.

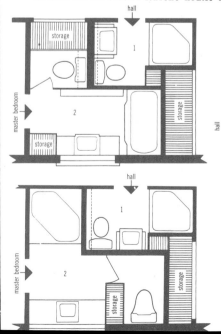

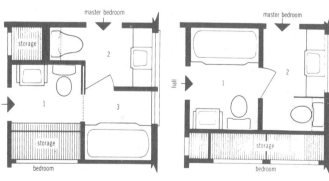

Here are four ways to lay out multiple bathroom facilities. By compacting the arrangements, several members of a family can make use of the rooms at one time. There is also the plumbing aspect to consider: Short lines will save money!

American-Standard

taken off the end of a bedroom, a space 36x96 inches being ample. You may even find that you have enough space for all three fixtures if you put the toilet at one end of the slice, the shower at the other, and the washbasin opposite the door at the middle. Some small washbasins are only 12 inches deep. If you are cramped for space, get a toilet that is smaller than standard. Shower stalls are commonly 30x30 inches.

The Inside Bathroom. Don't dismiss space as unusable just because it has no window. An inside bathroom, in many ways, is superior to one that has an exterior wall.

It is warmer. It is less drafty. It doesn't have the problem of condensation on windows. It is more private. It is quieter. With a good fan, its ventilation is superior. The fan should be connected so that it comes on with the light and has enough capacity to change air completely every 5 minutes. Put a grill in the lower part of the door or wall for incoming air, or take a slice off the bottom of the door.

If you want natural daylight in an inside

Snap a chalk line down center of bathroom's main area, and begin installation of cork floor tiles here. Though the felt is put down with linoleum paste, waterproof cement is required for tiles.

FIXTURE SIZES

BATHTUB:	Width:	Usually 31", but may be 30" or 32".
	Height:	14" to 16"
	Length:	Usually 54" or 60", but may also be 42" or 66". Square tubs are approximately 48" on a side.
TOILET:	Width:	Most tanks are 22½", but range is from 20" to 24".
	Height:	Usually 30". Range is from 18½" to 40".
	Depth:	Usually 30" from front of bowl to back of tank, but range is from 26" to 32".
	Clearance:	Need a minimum access of 18" x 30" at front. Also allow 30" for tank to give it some clearance on each side.
LAVATORY	Width:	Usual is 24", but may range from 12" to 36".
	Depth:	12" to 24" with 18" most popular. Corner style measures 12" to 19" on a side.
	Height:	31" is standard, but 34" to 36" is best when unit is for adult use only.
	Clearance:	Requires minimum access space of 18" x 24" at front.

New plastic drawers are easy to install, have steel runners, glide on smooth nylon pads. Any style front to match cabinet can be attached to drawer fronts. Plastic can never warp or stick.

bathroom, you may also be able to arrange that with a skylight. The skylight can include a ventilator built into its curb. It may also serve as a lighting fixture, so that round-the-clock light comes from the one source.

Structural Considerations. A bathroom and its equipment may add considerable weight to your house. You aren't likely to encounter any difficulties in this regard unless your floors are already sagging and shaky, or if you have to do some heavy notching of joists to accommodate plumbing pipes. Here's how you can save on weight: Apply ceramic tile with adhesive

Allow waterproof cement to dry five minutes before setting tile firmly in place over it. Use care to keep the cement off the tiles. Accidental smears can be wiped away very easily with a soapy rag.

Provide as much storage as you can in the bathroom. You can store not only toilet articles and linen here, but clothing as well. Corner storage cabinet needs to have room on only one side wall.

Cabinet has 4 different sizes of drawers below upper section of adjustable shelves. Unit is suspended off the floor to match the style of the adjoining off-the-floor vanity-lavatory as shown.

By attaching metal shelf standards for support of shelves, the placement of the shelves becomes completely flexible. Shelves are of plywood trimmed along front edge with thin wood strip.

instead of mortar. Use plastic wall, counter, and floor finishes. Use a steel tub and lavatory; they are lighter than cast iron.

In building storage, use new lightweight plastic drawers, such as those made by Washington Steel Products, Tacoma 1, Washington, and available at hardware and lumber dealers. They are not only feather light, but, made of high-impact polystyrene, are as rugged as they come.

If reinforcement of structure is essential, support first-floor joists by running a 4x10 beam as support under their center line. Second floor joists can be reinforced by spiking extra joists to existing ones. Ends of

these new joists should rest on bearing partitions. Sure, this does require opening up floor or ceiling, but you'll probably be doing that anyway for installation of pipes. Or if you drop the ceiling level in the floor below to give space for pipes, the extra supporting members can be installed here.

If your ceiling height is 8 feet or more, you'll also find definite advantages in dropping the bathroom ceiling to 7 feet. You can run pipes through the space, and the dead air pocket created will make the room both warmer and quieter. A new ceiling of acoustical tile, such as those made by Armstrong, is easy to install, inexpensive. •

7 ◊

Mini Bath & Laundry

OLD DOOR was removed and replaced by a window, freezer moved elsewhere in garage.

CEILING BEAMS were attached to garage roof rafters directly and with tie beams.

A SECOND bathroom is appreciated by a growing family. In some homes —especially those without basements— once the family has expanded there may be no room left to build another bath. We not only found the space, but added a laundry room for the wife, too.

Our mini bath and laundry were built into a 4x14-ft. area at the back of an oversized one-car garage. There is still plenty of room for the car and for storage of garden equipment. Most of the junk that previously took up this space has been thrown out, as it should have been years ago.

The first step is to draw up a floor plan. Take all configuration factors into consideration. Can you use an existing window or will you need a ventilating fan? What are your local building code requirements for both bathrooms and garages? Are there water and drain lines nearby? You may have to get the plan okayed by your local building department.

Next make up a materials list. This will give you a total cost estimate and help you to schedule work and stagger deliveries if necessary. We used 2x3 studs and framing, 2x6 floor joists and ceiling beams, ⅝-in. subflooring and ⅜-in. wallboard.

At this point it's a good idea to get bids and comments from plumbing contractors unless you will do the work yourself. Find out if the plumber can locate the sink, toilet and shower where you want them. If not, your plan must be modified. To save space, we used the smallest standard fixtures available: a 12x12-in. sink, a 32x32x78-in. shower stall and a close-coupled toilet measuring only 17 in. from the front of the bowl to the back of the tank. The sink and toilet tank were recessed into the walls to take up even less floor space.

Since the floor of the garage is about 18 in. lower than the house floor, it was necessary to build a new floor 18 in. high to allow room for the heating duct and to permit the various drain pipes to feed into the house waste lines. A foundation of cement blocks was built around the perimeter of the mini bath and 2x6 sills attached with anchor bolts. A layer of building felt must be placed between the top course of blocks and the sill.

A 2x6 joist header is nailed atop the sills. Floor joists, placed on 16-in. centers, butt up against this header. If any joists fall where plumbing lines or drains will come up through the floor, openings of the proper size must be framed with 2x6s.

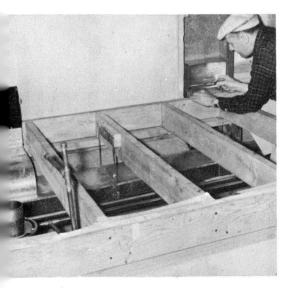

HEAT DUCTS and plumbing were run under elevated joists before the floor was laid.

SUBFLOOR was laid next, leaving framed openings for plumbing and access panels.

Mini Bath & Laundry

If you are not using a foundation and the floor of your bathroom will be right on the garage floor, you can bolt 2x3 or 2x4 sole plates (depending on the planned wall thickness) directly to the floor.

You are now ready to rough in plumbing, or have it done by a contractor. All lines, vents and drains are installed, but no fixtures are put in place. If you have warm air heating you can also install the ducts and registers at this point. When all the below-deck utilities are installed, you can nail down the subfloor.

Ceiling beams would normally be installed after the sidewall framing is in place but due to the construction of the garage roof in this case they were installed first. The 2x6 beams are hung from the roof rafters using short, vertical, 2x6 tie beams.

The easiest way to erect the sidewall is to cut the members to size, nail them together on the garage floor and erect whole sections at once. Frame up any

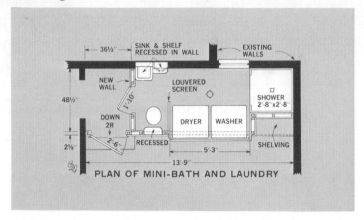

PLAN OF MINI-BATH AND LAUNDRY

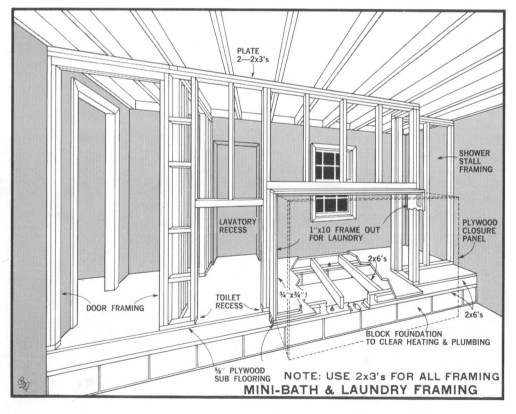

MINI-BATH & LAUNDRY FRAMING

ASSEMBLE, erect and then nail sidewalls in place. Note opening for toilet recess.

ACCESS PANEL for washer and dryer is easily removed for appliance maintenance.

openings you need for sink or toilet recesses, built-in cabinets or fan housings. Use temporary braces to hold the sidewall to the garage walls and roof rafters, then nail the sole plate to the subfloor.

You can now install the wiring for lights and outlets or have the work done by a qualified electrician.

Assemble the stall shower next. It is erected inside an alcove lined with water-resistant wallboard. All needed parts are delivered in a carton with instructions and the thing goes together like an Erector Set. The pan goes over the previously-installed drain and the walls are put in place and fastened together. Then connect the supply lines to the faucets.

Fiberglass insulation is stapled between the studs and, after the ceiling is in place, laid between the ceiling beams. The walls and ceiling are covered with 4x8-ft. wallboard. At this point you can cover the subfloor with a plywood floor. If you want access panels to get at the plumbing in case of leaks, these should be cut to fit framing installed when the joists were cut.

The washer and dryer were installed through the access panel in the wall. This removable panel allows maintenance chores to be performed without wrestling the appliances out into the middle of the floor. The panel rests on a small ledge and is held in place by butterfly fasteners. A vent system of plastic and aluminum tube was hooked up. Clamps on the plastic tube make it possible to remove the vent when the access panel is opened.

Install the sink and toilet fixtures. A recessed medicine cabinet with louvered doors was built in over the sink.

A 34-in. wide door was hung at the entrance and trim moldings around door, window, sink recess and cabinets fitted and nailed in place. A louvered panel was fastened between the toilet and dryer with small metal angles. Paint, wallpaper and lighting fixtures finished the job. Had we been able to reverse the position of the sink-toilet group and the washer-dryer group, a sliding door could give bath privacy while the laundry was in use. The new window prevented this. —*Bill Duggan* •

Modernizing an Old W.C.

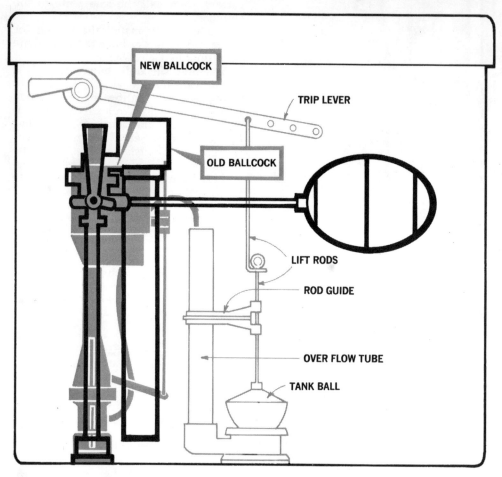

NEW BALLCOCK

TRIP LEVER

OLD BALLCOCK

LIFT RODS

ROD GUIDE

OVER FLOW TUBE

TANK BALL

SPACE-AGE MATERIALS and completely new design change the age-old toilet tank ball cock mechanism to a modern design that works on the flow of water rather than its level.

SPACE AGE materials and design have, at long last, caught up with the generations-old toilet tank. While there have been many variations in the design and materials used, toilet tanks over the years have all worked on the same principle—the level of the water in the tank shuts off the flow.

Now a new design uses the flow of water to operate the valve rather than the level. Coupled with modern plastics and stainless steel pipes and seats, this design should solve the minor, but annoying and sometimes expensive,

problem of the leaky or noisy toilet tank. More interesting still—in this day of ever rising inflation—it does it with a new mechanism that doesn't cost an arm and a leg. The cost is less than $5 and it take less time—and a lot less knowhow—to install the Fluidmaster 200 shown here than it does to fiddle around with an old ball cock mechanism and coax it back into operation.

Toilet tank problems are caused by corrosion and mechanical wear. Fiddling with a half-understood mechanism often makes them worse. Then comes

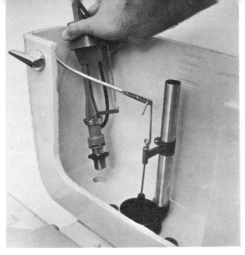

FLUIDMASTER BALL COCK SHANK fits any tank replacing ball cock, float arm and ball.

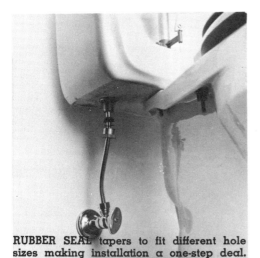

RUBBER SEAL tapers to fit different hole sizes making installation a one-step deal.

RUBBER HOSE refill tube must be above overflow pipe when tank is full to fill bowl.

the plumber—if, when and eventually —to fix the tank and present his rarely modest bill. When he's done your 19th century gadget is fine again.

The recently designed Fluidmaster 200 replaces the ball cock (which seeps, fails to shut off completely, or just plain runs-on until you twiddle the flush handle), float arm (which can get bent out of adjustment) and the float ball (which can leak and thereby fail to shut off the water flow at the correct level).

An inverted plastic cup slides up and down a plastic post to signal when the tank is full. It actuates the flow of water to shut itself off. The result is that the tank fills more quickly and then shuts off all at once instead of bit by bit. Should anything go wrong, the tank will not seep or dribble continually. It runs full-out in fits and starts so you cannot help but know that there is trouble. Dirt in the valve is the usual cause and the cure is simple. An eighth of a turn frees the mechanism so you can flush it out and reassemble it just as easily.

To put in a Fluidmaster ball cock, shut off the flow of water and drain the tank. Sponge the bottom dry to prevent spills on the floor. Then remove the old ball cock assembly by unscrewing the fittings on the under side of the tank. Replace it with the new one. Tapered rubber sealing gaskets solve the problem of different sized mounting holes. Do not overtighten the pipe coupling as you might crack the tank. Its rubber seal will not leak as long as the ball cock is firmly in place.

The refill tube, made of black rubber instead of fracture-prone metal, mounts on the ball cock and is held in place above the overflow pipe with a stainless steel clip.

That's all there is to it. Hold down the float when filling the tank for the first cycle to fill the cup with water. Sliding the cup up or down adjusts the water level in the tank.

Fluidmaster 200 is available in most hardware and plumbing supply stores or can be ordered from its maker, Fluidmaster Inc., 1800 Via Burton, Anaheim, Calif. 92806 for about $4.25. For areas with plumbing codes that require anti-siphon ball cocks, there's the model 400 for a suggested retail price of $6.00. •

One-Handle Faucet

ONE HAND is all you need to adjust water temperature: a big kitchen aid.

FOR added convenience in the kitchen, there is nothing like a single-handle faucet. Push the handle straight back and mixed water of moderate temperature rushes from the nozzle. Tip the handle to the left and the stream of water gets hotter; tip it to the right and the water gets colder. The water temperature can be quickly adjusted using only one hand. After trying it you will realize what a nuisance the conventional faucet is.

The installation is quick and simple. After turning off the water supply, disconnect and remove the pipes from the old faucet. They are usually held with compression fittings. Simply back off the nut to free the tubing.

A basin wrench is used to reach up under the sink and undo the flanged nuts holding the old faucet to the deck. Scrape away the old putty and clean the deck. Then lay in a bed of fresh putty as shown in the bottom photo.

Insert compression fittings into the ends of the inlet pipes. Place the rubber gasket onto the bed of putty, centering the holes over those in the sink. Carefully insert the faucet, centering it over the gasket. Tighten the flanged nuts and connect the compression fittings.

Single-handle faucets are available for showers and tubs too. Leading manufacturers are American Standard, Peerless Faucet Co. and the Delta Co. •

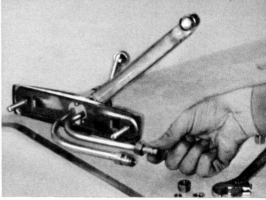

ATTACH FITTINGS to new faucet tubing. Tubing is straightened later if necessary.

RUBBER GASKET sits on a thick bed of fresh putty. Faucet just slips into place.

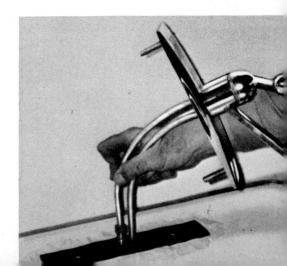

New Bathroom for Old

By Lou Rubsamen

IF you've toyed with the idea of doing major remodeling surgery on a bathroom, be assured that it's well worth the effort. The remodeled bathroom we show here was no cake walk for me to do—but it didn't try my soul, either. And for about $600 I got myself new and modern everything—tub, sink, toilet, walls, floor . . . plus some built-in accessories that provide new convenience without robbing valuable space from the pint-size 5x6 ft. room.

Here's how I did it and some tips I picked up along the way.

Probably the hardest part of the job was removing the fixtures. Or, I should say, the tub. The sink and toilet were simply lifted off wall brackets and the toilet unbolted from the floor. But the tub, though small, definitely was not shaped for carrying and its size belied its weight: it must have been over 300 lbs. My only advice: get some strong friends.

Before removing it we stripped the walls of old tileboard and WW II-vintage composition board down to bare studs and took up the linoleum, exposing a bare wooden floor.

With frosty mornings on my mind, we stapled new insulation—aluminum batts—between studs on the two outside walls. We then framed for the accessories.

Next, the new tub (just as hernia-threatening as the old one) was installed on a horizontal cleat and the plumbing connected. Plumbing-wise, there's nothing to be afraid of with any of the fixtures. If you pay attention when you take the old ones out, you won't have trouble installing the new ones. These are available in standard sizes—made to go in the same places the old ones came out of. If new piping is needed—for example, we wanted higher faucets for the tub—you can use short lengths of copper and standard fittings;

NEWSPAPER over flour-water mixture provides protection for new tub during work.

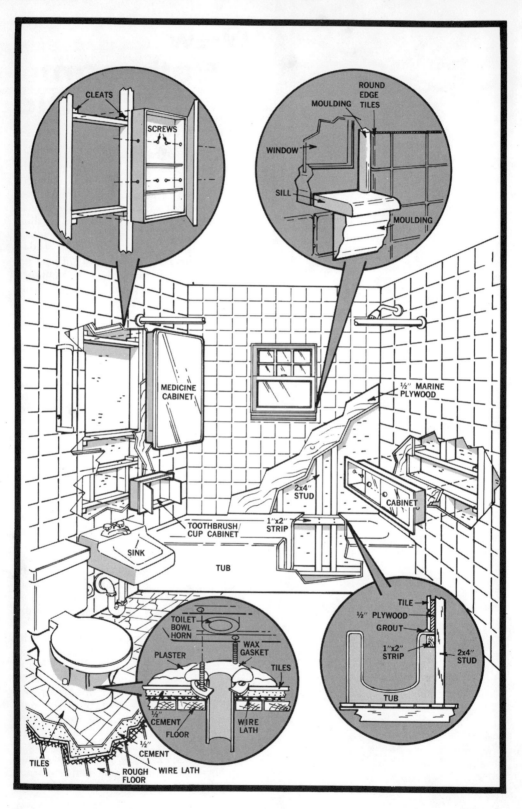

solder is sufficient for sealing joints.

I nailed a good grade of ½-in. marine plywood to the studs, first sawing cutouts for the accessories.

We chose bright aqua ceramic tile for the walls. These are installed by laying on a bed of adhesive with a toothed trowel, then pressing the tile in place. The tiles, each 4x4 in., have lips on the edges and self-space. After allowing them to dry for a couple of days, you swab grout into the joints. The excess is removed with a sponge. A piece of burlap did a good job removing the dry film that forms. After cleaning the grout with an abrasive cleanser, a sealer is applied to prevent yellowing.

When tiling, it's best to work from the ground up. If you expect to take only a few days to do the job, a rented tile cutter is a good investment for cutting tiles to fit around the windows, accessory openings etc. A pair of nippers is handy for nibbling tiles to fit around pipes and the like. Grout and trim plates are used to hide the ragged edges.

For neatness, plan to have a line of grout run along the wall-ceiling joint, unless you want to tile the ceiling. We didn't because of fear that upstairs traffic might vibrate the tile loose onto someone's head. Rather, we simply gave our ceiling two coats of sand paint. Its sandy finish effectively hides hairline cracks, bumps, etc.

With the tile up, the toilet was put in, a matter of dropping in a new wax gasket and laying the toilet on a ring of wet plaster before bolting it in place. Toilet tank and sink were then hung on special wall brackets provided with them. Freeform tile was laid on the floor.

Final step was installing the accessories. We chose all chrome ones—a toothbrush and cup cabinet, toilet and tissue paper dispensers and an extra medicine chest. These were slipped into the recesses and fastened to the framing by running screws through predrilled holes. Hanging a towel ring completed the job.

Oh, one final bit of advice: Don't forget to turn off the water before you begin. •

AFTER installing new wax gasket, a bed of wet plaster is troweled on and the new toilet is seated in it, then bolted in place.

SPECIAL bracket makes hanging sink simple. Bracket is screwed to studs or plywood panelling and sink hangs on by its own weight. If you like, you can fasten it.

7 Bathroom Repairs Anyone Can Do

PLUMBING may not be the most glamorous of the skills required by the modern homeowner, but it is one of the more essential. If you have ever had to pester a plumber for a month or so to come to your house and charge you $15.02 to replace a 2¢ faucet washer, you know why. If your problem is more serious—a burst pipe, say, or a toilet that won't fill and therefore can't be used—try to get the neighborhood plumber to come right over on an emergency basis. It's like trying to get your doctor to make a house call, except that you can't very easily pack up your plumbing system and take it to his office.

The maze of piping and fixtures that makes up a home's plumbing system need not terrify even a ten-thumbed do-it-yourselfer. The basic care and repairs that will keep the system functioning are quite simple, and economical too, since most involve only minimal expense—if you shortcut the hefty labor bill of the professional plumber.

1. Leaky faucets. This plagues everyone at one time or another, no matter how good the home's plumbing system. In almost all cases, the cause is wear of the washer that fits over the valve opening. Although there are differences in faucets, the basic repair—replacement of the washer—is the same.

First step is to turn off the supply of water to the faucet. In most cases, there will be a valve on the water line near the faucet. If not, trace back along the system to find a shutoff point. If nowhere else, you can turn off the entire system at the meter or wherever the water enters your house. (It is a good idea to note the location of this main valve and to acquaint all members of the family with it for emergency purposes.)

Next, remove the screw that holds the faucet handle in place. Underneath this is a bonnet or cap nut that is also removed. (Wrap a cloth or tape around chrome fittings to prevent damage from wrenches.) Now you should be able to

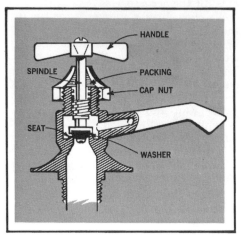

X-RAY view of faucet. A variety of maladies can beset it, all, fortunately, easily curable.

unscrew and lift out the entire spindle. If not, slip the handle back on and use it for leverage.

With the spindle removed, examination will disclose the worn or tattered rubber washer at the bottom, held in place by a brass screw. Remove the screw and washer and replace with similar items. An assortment of various-sized faucet washers along with replacement screws can be found in any hardware store, costing 20 to 50 cents. Reverse the procedure to put the faucet back together.

But what if, after you reassemble the faucet and turn the water back on, your faucet still "drip . . . drip . . . drip" or, worse yet, "drip.drip.drip.drip.drip.drip.drip."? Don't despair. If the faucet has seen considerable wear—you've already replaced several washers—the seat inside the faucet body against which the washer rests may be worn.

Go back to the hardware store, this time to pick up a special seat-dressing tool called a reamer. There are several types available—you should be able to get one to suit your porposes for under $1. Turn off the water and again remove the spindle. Insert the tool into the faucet body and follow the manufacturer's directions for dressing or smoothing the seat. Hold the tool vertically during the operation. This should solve your problem.

Now if a faucet or valve leaks around the spindle, new packing is probably needed. Simply remove the cap nut and scrape out the old packing. Install a new packing washer, or wrap strands of graphite-asbestos wicking around the spindle. Now turn the cap down tight against the spindle. No more leak! Until next time.

2. Toilet tank doesn't refill. Water closet or toilet tank mechanisms vary in design, but general instructions can be given for pinpointing and correcting problems. Probably the most common complaint is that the tank does not refill but water keeps running into the bowl. Since this precludes flushing the toilet, the problem can be somewhat acute. The cause is usually the failure of the

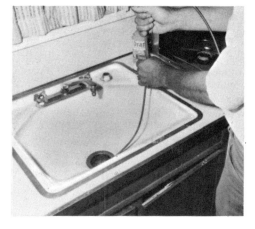

LEAKY faucet is usually due to worn washer. You'll find this at the bottom of spindle.

SNAKE is good tool for clearing all types of drains. It can probe deeply into pipe.

LEAKY copper pipe can be resoldered if accessible. Pipe must be completely dry.

IF toilet tank doesn't refill, culprit is likely to be worn rubber ball valve. Replace it.

tank ball to fit on its seat properly.

The tank ball is a hollow rubber ball—it comes in a variety of shapes—that sits in the opening at the bottom of the tank to shut off the flow of water to the toilet bowl. If it has become soft or misshapen simply unscrew it from its lift wire and install a new one (you may need a new lift wire, too; both items are at the hardware store). A bent lift wire or one that binds in its guides may also prevent the ball from seating properly. Check to see that it drops easily into place, and straighten the wire and guides as necessary. Still another reason for the ball's not seating properly could be that the metal around the seat itself is worn. This can be smoothed with emery cloth.

3. Water runs with tank filled. Another common toilet-tank complaint is that the water continues to run after the tank is filled, with the excess escaping through the overflow. This does not prevent the toilet from functioning, but it is annoying, and can be expensive if your water is metered. This problem could be caused by a leaky float ball —the brass or plastic ball that rises with the water level in the tank. Lift up the float. If

the water stops running, but starts up again as you release the float and it sinks down, replace the float by unscrewing it from the end of the float rod.

If the water continues to run even when you lift up the float ball, the problem may be a worn float valve (intake valve) at the other end of the rod from the ball. You may be able to coax some more service out of it by bending the float rod down at the ball end. This puts more force on the valve to shut off the water flow. Or you can try replacing the washer on the valve. Beyond doing this, you need a plumber.

4. Sluggish drains. Getting rid of water and waste can be as troublesome as getting it to where you want it. Drains can become clogged by objects dropped into them or by accumulations of grease

While a toilet tank is more complicated than a faucet, it still doesn't present overwhelming repair problems, as the text indicates.

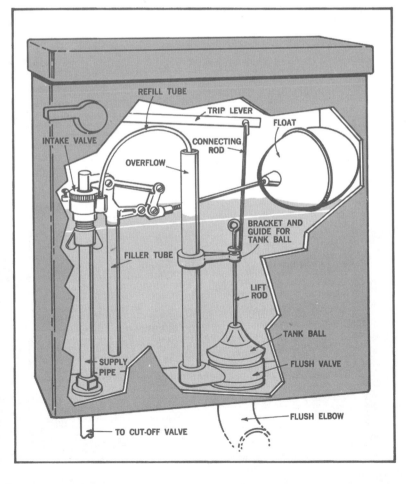

REFILL TUBE
TRIP LEVER
FLOAT
INTAKE VALVE
CONNECTING ROD
OVERFLOW
BRACKET AND GUIDE FOR TANK BALL
FILLER TUBE
LIFT ROD
TANK BALL
SUPPLY PIPE
FLUSH VALVE
FLUSH ELBOW
TO CUT-OFF VALVE

or dirt. If a drain is merely sluggish, try pouring in a chemical cleaner, following the manufacturer's direction to the letter. Be very careful when using these cleaners, and if any spills on your hands or clothing, wash away immediately with cold water. And never use such a cleaner in a completely stopped drain, as it must reach the obstruction to be effective.

5. Stopped-up drains. When a drain is stopped completely, a plunger or "plumber's friend" may come to the rescue. When using a plunger in a sink or toilet bowl, make sure that the rubber end is covered by the water to insure proper suction. Work the tool vigorously and deliberately—not too fast. Give it about 10 or 12 strokes, then allow water to run off. If still clogged, repeat. It takes time for this process to work, so don't give up too easily. Repeat the procedure eight or nine times. Each time you stop plunging, there will be a backwash into the bowl. Remove hairpins, paper, or other solid objects that may be sucked up.

Another unclogger is a snake—a long, flexible, twisted steel wire. Most types have a metal handle that is moved further and further back along the snake as it is worked into the drain. Various sizes are available at the hardware store.

If there is a cleanout plug in the trap below the clogged drain, remove it and work the snake in from there, first placing a pan or other container underneath so that the water in the pipe will not spill on the floor. Run the snake in as far as it will go, then remove it. Replace the plug, and pour boiling water into the drain. If it runs through freely, your problem is over.

But, if the household gods are frowning on your efforts, go back to the snake and repeat the process. If that still doesn't do the trick, head for the basement and the main drainpipe, looking for cleanout plugs in this line. Remove these and run the snake through in both directions as far as possible. Still no luck? Sorry pal, but it's time to call in the pro.

If your home suffers from chronic disorders of the waste system, the plumbing was probably poorly designed to begin with. To prevent frequent calls for the plumber, use a chemical solvent at regular intervals. Follow manufacturer's recommendations regarding frequency. But remember not to use this product when there is a complete stoppage.

6. Leaky pipes. These usually call for the services of a professional. Pipe clamps can help in an emergency. These consist of two pieces of metal with a rubber liner; they are attached around the pipe by screws. Get a supply from the hardware store, including at least one for each size pipe in your system.

If you are caught without clamps, friction or plastic tape wrapped around the leak may slow or even stop it. A rubber patch under the tape will make it more effective. Even a wood or metal screw inserted into a hole may hold temporarily. Turning off the water makes it easier.

Vibration sometimes causes leaks at pipe joints. In threaded steel pipe, this can usually be repaired by applying joint compound. On copper tubing, the joint can be cleaned and resoldered if it is accessible. The water must first be turned off and drained from the tubing, which must be dry before it can be heated to soldering temperature. Apply flux to the joint, then solder. Remember, when soldering, to heat the workpiece, not the solder.

7. Frozen water pipes. In cold weather, water may freeze in pipes, especially in unheated crawl spaces or basements. Since water expands when it freezes, there is a good chance that it will rupture the pipe. Insulation may be used to slow down the freezing, but this is not completely dependable. Electric heating cables wrapped around a pipe will keep it from freezing; they are the best method for thawing water that has already frozen in a pipe.

Another effective thawing method is to cover the pipe with rags, then pour hot water over the rags. Whichever method is used, first open a faucet and start thawing at that point. This will permit steam to escape, avoiding a buildup of potentially dangerous pressure in the pipe. Make sure that steam does not condense and refreeze before it reaches the faucet.

A blowtorch should never be used for thawing. It may heat the water to such a point that sufficient steam is generated to rupture the pipe, releasing the scalding steam. The frozen pipe is problem enough without looking for more. •

Building a Bay Window

by George Daniels

It's easy and inexpensive if you plan the job carefully

IF YOU'D like a brighter living room with the feeling of much greater space, and you'd like it on a small budget, the chances are a bay window is your answer. In a typical small home it can add enough space to keep dining area from crowding living room, and its large room-brightening glass area creates the impression of a considerably larger room. Yet, unlike a major room extension it doesn't require a costly pile of materials nor a lengthy construction job. And the room to which it is added can remain in use during the work.

Check on the practical factors before you decide on the size or location of your bay window. For a first step, look in your basement to see if any major plumbing (like drain or soil pipes) runs through the wall area you want to open up. If so, get an estimate from your plumber on shifting the pipes. This can be a big cost-booster and may not even be practical. Your best bet in that event is another window location.

If the window is to be in a nonsupporting wall, the job will be a little simpler as a heavy header across the top of the wall

Photos here show house with and without bay window. Bay window replaces four lower windows, as photo shows. Addition brightens living room, adds about 4 feet to length.

First step is to dig trench below frost line for concrete footing of bay window foundation. Small opening is made through house wall to assure accurate matching of floor level of room and window. You can buy concrete you'll need by cubic yard.

No form is needed for footing. Ready-mix truck delivers concrete, chutes it into trench. Like water in trough, wet concrete tends to level itself, but must be checked with mason's level, trowled to flat upper surface, ready for masonry's blocks.

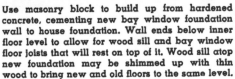

Use masonry block to build up from hardened concrete, cementing new bay window foundation wall to house foundation. Wall ends below inner floor level to allow for wood sill and bay window floor joists that will rest on top of it. Wood sill atop new foundation may be shimmed up with thin wood to bring new and old floors to the same level.

Wood sill and plywood subfloor are installed. Outside wall surface (siding and sheathing) have been cut away below windows, exposing inside wall. Bottom of inside wall has also been opened for 1 or 2 inches above floor level to permit new window subfloor to be slipped, nailed into place. Bay window floor joists run across new foundation.

opening won't be needed, and the room ceiling may be continued smoothly into the bay window area. If you're opening a supporting wall, you'll need a larger header or girder across the top of the opening to support the portion of the floor above that which was previously supported by the wall. This isn't much added expense but it usually calls for a visible beam (which can be made decorative) or a lower ceiling level in the bay window.

An easy way to tell one type wall from the other: a nonsupporting wall runs parallel to the joists or beams in the floor above. You can check in the attic or even in the basement, as joists in upper and lower floors usually run in the same direction. Outside walls that run at right angles to the floor joists above them are supporting walls.

Exposure and view are the other major location factors. Naturally, you'll favor the best-view location if practicable, though shrubbery may be used when practical considerations make a less favorable location necessary. As to exposure, favor north or east if summer heat is a major problem. If it isn't, a bay window facing west will

brighten your living room at cocktail time and even through dinner on summer evenings. In cool climates a window to the south affords the greatest overall sunlight throughout the day. A shade tree in line with it is an ideal combination, as summer foliage blocks direct sun in hot weather; bare branches let it pass in winter.

If you plan to build your own bay window, you'll save work by planning it with a rectangular floor plan. If you're set on the traditional angular form, however, a portable circular saw like the one shown in the photos, will minimize the extra work of angle cutting on rafters and other framing parts.

To keep costs down, plan your job around standard window sizes. For sake of appearance be sure that the muntins and sash parts (particularly along horizontal lines) of adjacent windows align.

You can assure weathertightness and maximum strength by using plyscore for sheathing, subfloor, and roof, while cutting labor on these parts to a minimum. Because of the large glass area, three or four standard 4x8 panels are enough for a moderate sized bay window.

Here is typical framing around a small window in conventional house wall. Note arrangement of uprights at window ends to support header beam at top of window, which, in turn, supports short uprights from the top of window to top of wall.

To enlarge wall opening for bay window installation, framing is altered like this. Horizontal "sill" piece across opening has been removed to let floor run through it. Large header beam across top of opening provides support for floor above, previously supported by intermediate uprights or studs. This is necessary when opening is made in "supporting" wall. If it's non-supporting wall header can usually be omitted, giving full ceiling height in the bay window.

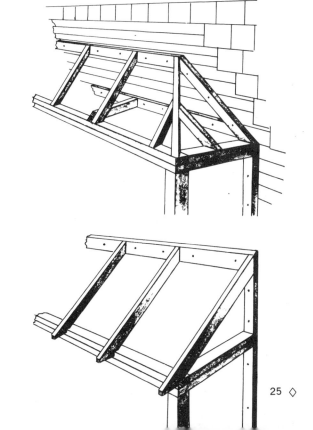

Here's how hip-type angled roof framing is laid out. Rear members are nailed to existing house wall. Only one ceiling joist is shown (center) in bay window framing. Finished structure should have them on 16-inch centers, the same as in the house.

Simplest type of bay window roof framing is possible if bay window is rectangular in form, like the one shown here. Saves work, material.

Wall framing now goes up. House siding (shingles) are removed 2 feet above bay window framing to nail new framing directly to house sheathing and framing. Roof of bay window starts about a foot above top of framing shown here, and slopes down.

The windows are now fitted carefully, and trim is installed, as shown in photograph above. Plank temporarily closes opening along bottom of inner wall at floor level. Living room is still usable as work progresses. Cloth could cover work area.

The large glass area leaves little interior wall area not covered by trim. In a typical installation this means few, if any, wallboard joints to spackle except at corners, where the job's easy even for an amateur. The small wall area also lets you use the best grade of insulation between walls without much increase in cost. Usually the ceiling can be covered with a single wallboard panel, requiring only a single seam to spackle at the bay window-room juncture.

To eliminate the need for a time-consuming finishing job on the finish flooring in the bay window area buy it prefinished. As you'd need to buy the finishing materials, in addition to unfinished flooring, the difference in overall cost is slight, the saving in time and work is great. And you're assured of a professional appearance.

Most of the bay window framing consists of stock 2x4's, even for roof rafters, as the span is seldom more than four or five feet. The joists that support the floor, however, should in most instances be the same size as those in the adjoining house floor. Although lighter joists would usually be more than adequate, you'll save trouble by matching them to the house joists size, as you'll find it much easier to bring floor levels flush with each other. Simply build the bay window foundation up to the same height as the house foundation and use the same type of sill and joists. Usually it will be easier to run the bay window floor joists parallel to the house wall, with ends supported on the new foundation, even though the span might be a little shorter if they ran inward to the house.

For a first-hand look at the construction details that will go into your bay window have a look at the sill atop the foundation walls in your basement and the roof rafters in your attic, assuming you haven't done an interior finishing job in these areas of your house. The next best bet: look over any new home construction job in the framing stage. You'll see that you can do the work with ordinary hand tools, though a power saw will speed the job on the more elaborate designs.

Windows are now permanently installed, new siding shingles are on house and bay window. They will be stained to match rest of house. Metal flashing is installed under lowest course of shingles above bay window roof, and led out over start of roofing to prevent rain seepage at juncture. Now that bay window is completely weathertight, inner wall separating it from living room wall is removed. Header at top of opening through wall had been installed previously. Finished window adds distinction to house.

If you need help in visualizing your basic design use large sheets of wrapping paper Scotch-taped together to permit a full-sized pencil outline of your floor plan, or use several joined strips of building paper like Tanskin for the same purpose. You can pencil in the location of studs, based on the window sizes you plan to use, and work out the rest of your framing from there. You can choose the window sizes from a wide selection at your lumber-yard, and get standard ready-made screens and storm windows to match if you want them.

If you're casually handy with tools, the job on an average sized bay window shouldn't take more than two weekends of spare time, and you won't have to open your existing house wall until the bay window unit has been made weathertight. •

cantilevered
CHILD'S BED

Dadoes in bed frame can be cut on jointer-planer (note Duro safety guard), table saw.

Below left, special bit countersinks for screw head and drills tapered hole in one operation. Part being drilled here is plywood bottom; it's glued, screwed to frame.

Below, legs are screwed in place. No glue is used so that bed can be disassembled.

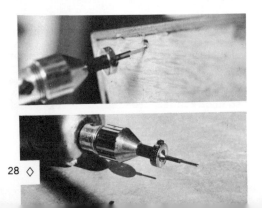

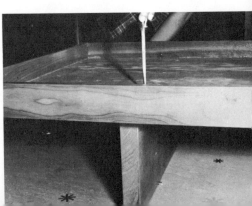

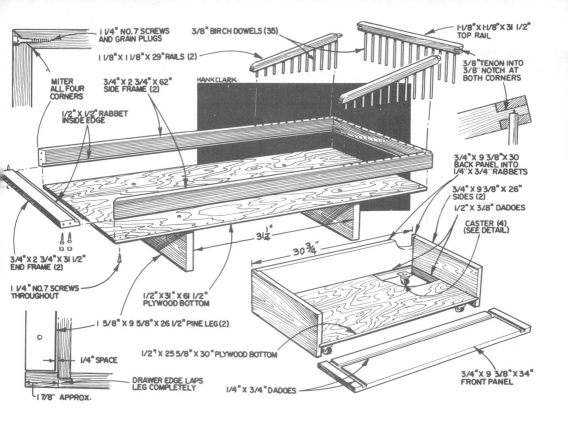

Simple, modern, this bed also provides toy or storage space.

By Harold Kelly

SIMPLE construction, modern styling and a sturdy result are the virtues of this bed. And just as important is the storage drawer built in underneath, easy to pull out for use as a toy chest. The bed shown here is 5 feet long, for a 3-year-old, but the author also built a full-size one for his oldest child; in that one the drawer serves for blanket storage.

Construction took less than 8 hours, and cost can be as low as $10, without mattress. The frame is solid cherry, head rail is ash, bed and drawer bottom are ½-in. plywood, drawer sides are ¾-in. thick pine, bed legs are simply fir 2x10's.

The ¾x2¾-in. cherry frame has a ½-in. dado cut in the bottom edge to receive the plywood bottom. The corners are cut at a 45-degree angle and glued and screwed together, using two 1¼-in. No. 7 screws at each corner (same size screws are used throughout project).

Cut the legs to size and screw them in place. These 2x10's can be bought at a local lumberyard—but note that they actually will measure 1⅝x9⅝ in. Cut the drawer sides from ¾x10-in. shelving (which will also measure 9⅝ in. wide). Reduce this width to 9⅜ in. to afford sufficient clearance for the drawer to roll in and out without binding. Buy the rollers that are to be screwed to the drawer bottom *before* you cut dadoes in the drawer sides. Reason is that the rollers should protrude about ⅛ in. below the bottom of the drawer sides, and roller sizes vary; therefore you'll have to locate the drawer bottom to suit. The free-rolling casters used here cost 15c apiece. A simple brass door handle was used for the drawer.

The headboard is designed so that there are no sharp corners for the child to roll into while tossing in his sleep.

Headboard rails are bored to receive the ⅜-in. thick birch dowels at proper angle.

Here, back of headboard rail is drilled. Without drill press, make jig to get angle.

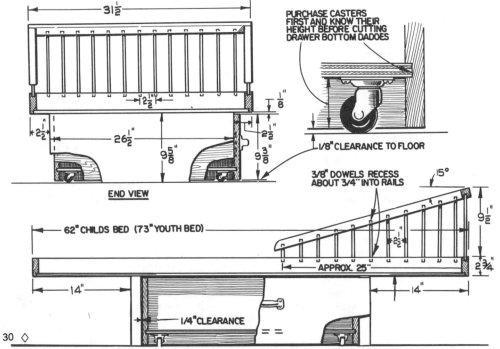

PURCHASE CASTERS FIRST AND KNOW THEIR HEIGHT BEFORE CUTTING DRAWER BOTTOM DADOES

1/8" CLEARANCE TO FLOOR

END VIEW

3/8" DOWELS RECESS ABOUT 3/4" INTO RAILS

15°

62" CHILDS BED (73" YOUTH BED)

APPROX. 25"

1/4" CLEARANCE

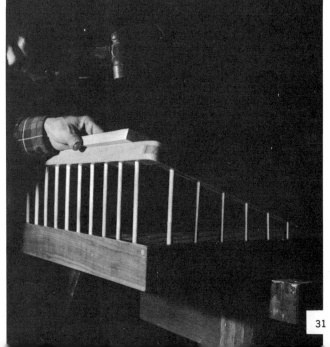

Birch dowels are spaced 2½ in. on centers and marked off on frame before holes are drilled. Hole in side of jig is used to space the holes evenly. Headboard is all assembled at this point.

Dowels on headboard are aligned with holes in frame. Then merely force-fit the dowels in place, without use of glue. Use scrap block under hammer to avoid mark.

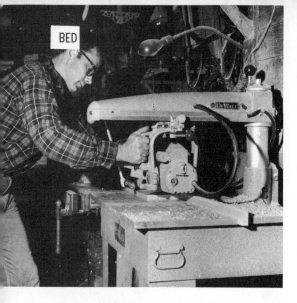

Drawer sides are cut and dadoed with table saw—preferably with overhead radial saw.

Drawer bottom is positioned so that rollers protrude ⅛ in. below drawer sides.

The head rail is made of 1¼x1¼-in. ash, but only because it was on hand—cherry, oak or any hardwood will do as well. Refer to the drawings on preceding pages for the proper size and angle of the head rail.

The ⅜-in. birch dowels were spaced 2½ in. on centers. The holes are drilled in the head rail after it is cut to size and assembled—a drill press is real handy for getting the angles just right. If you don't have a drill press, the same type of jig that was used to help drill the holes in the bed frame (see photo) can be used with the head rail. Dowels are

fitted into the head rail and then trimmed to size.

Finally, the headboard unit is fitted into the bed frame and forced into place. For a finish, the whole unit was given three coats of Fabulon, smoothed down with steel wool between coats. If you don't care to make your own foam-rubber mattress, one can be bought for around $38, complete with zippered cover. Foam rubber is a good bet, since a good grade will assure you of no sag in the middle or the usual mattress troubles due to the young one jumping in bed. •

Toy-or-storage drawer slides out easily, contributes to a neat, clutter-free bedroom.

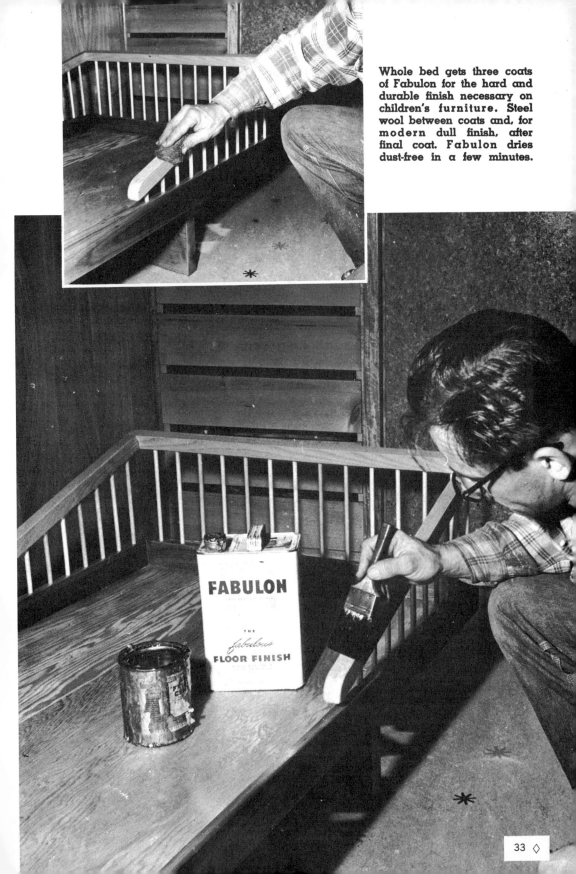

Whole bed gets three coats of Fabulon for the hard and durable finish necessary on children's furniture. Steel wool between coats and, for modern dull finish, after final coat. Fabulon dries dust-free in a few minutes.

FABULON

THE *fabulous* FLOOR FINISH

A Child's Bedroom

A complete suite for the youngsters, with a place for everything.

ALTHOUGH these units were actually made to completely furnish a young fellow's room, without having to lay out money for ready-made pieces, the designs are such that the young people will find them practical way up into their teens. And many a grown-up will find his room made more livable by units such as this, modified to suit his tastes and pursuits.

A room does not have to be large to have so many built-ins. The sample floor plan shown is for a bedroom no more than 10x10 feet. All the projects are dimensioned to suit this size room. So if the room you have in mind is this size—give or take a foot in either direction—you can work right from the plans provided. The work top, of course, can be as long as needed or there is room for. Some cabinets can be added underneath this to provide drawer space close to the work-top, or possibly a shallow drawer to hold the writing tools needed at a desk.

Before you start construction, make your own floor plan—a very simple one, but drawing it to scale. Then make scaled cut-outs of the projects shown here and place them on the layout, moving them about until you have arrived at an arrangement that makes the most of available space and which provides as much open area as possible. Traffic patterns in a bedroom are not critical but don't neglect enough room around a bed so friend wife won't have to struggle to prepare it, and enough room in front of the work-top or desk so a chair can be placed there.

If possible, arrange the work area to get light from an existing window. Leave the most open floor space near the entrance door. Don't place projects so doors opening into the room will bang into them. Remember that built-ins become part of the house and you can't take them with you when you go. If this idea doesn't appeal to you, make the projects as units that can be moved around and do not attach to walls.

Wardrobe

Start this off by cutting the three main, vertical panels to overall size and notching them at the base for the toe space. Follow with the floor frames (B and C) and the ceiling frames (E and F). Erect one panel, set in one floor frame (which can be assembled as a separate unit). Then follow with the second panel, the second floor frame and then the last panel. Floor frames can be nailed to the floor; the panels to the frames. Add the ceiling frames, driving a few nails through them into the ceiling joists if possible.

When erecting these three panels, work with a level and a square to be sure the panels are plumb and perfectly parallel to each other. This will pay off later when it comes to hanging doors and fitting in drawer fronts.

Next, install all your shelves. Make and install the drawer frames. Install these very carefully so that all the drawer parts (drawers are identical) can be cut on a production basis. In fact, it wouldn't be a bad idea to make a spacer block having the same dimensions as a drawer front, and use it to space the drawer frames correctly;

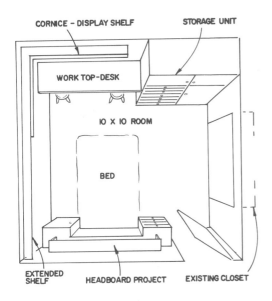

CORNICE - DISPLAY SHELF   STORAGE UNIT

WORK TOP-DESK

IO X IO ROOM

BED

EXTENDED SHELF   HEADBOARD PROJECT   EXISTING CLOSET

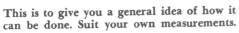

This is to give you a general idea of how it can be done. Suit your own measurements.

Keep in mind that every inch of space should be utilized, even the shelf over the cornice.

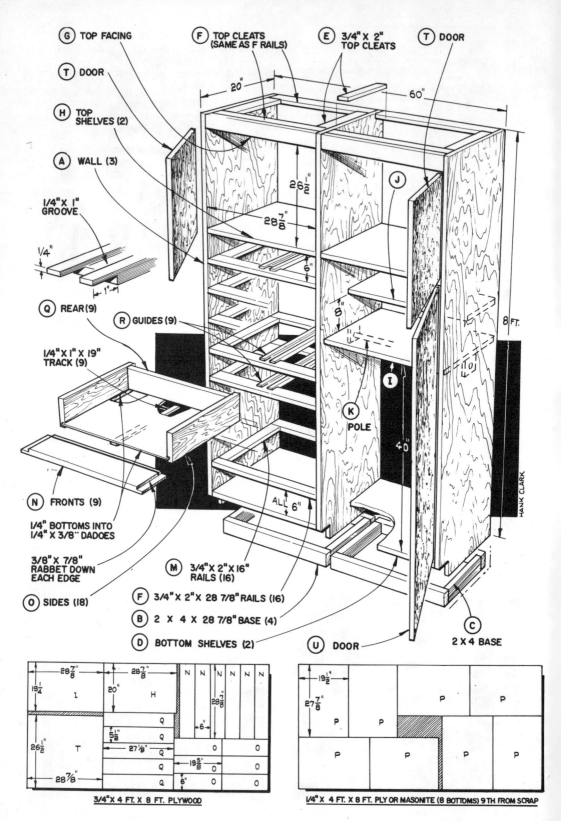

G TOP FACING

F TOP CLEATS (SAME AS F RAILS)

E 3/4" X 2" TOP CLEATS

T DOOR

T DOOR

H TOP SHELVES (2)

A WALL (3)

1/4" X 1" GROOVE

1/4"

1"

Q REAR (9)

R GUIDES (9)

1/4" X 1" X 19" TRACK (9)

N FRONTS (9)

1/4" BOTTOMS INTO 1/4" X 3/8" DADOES

3/8" X 7/8" RABBET DOWN EACH EDGE

O SIDES (18)

M 3/4" X 2" X 16" RAILS (16)

F 3/4" X 2" X 28 7/8" RAILS (16)

B 2 X 4 X 28 7/8" BASE (4)

D BOTTOM SHELVES (2)

U DOOR

C 2 X 4 BASE

J

K POLE

I

20"

60"

26 1/2"

28 7/8"

6"

8"

5"

10"

40"

8 FT.

ALL 6"

HANK CLARK

28 7/8"   28 7/8"
19 1/4"   20"
I   H
N N N N N N
26 1/2"
T
27 1/8"
Q
Q
Q
Q
Q
O O
O O
O O
6"
1 1/2"
19 5/8"
28 7/8"
6"

3/4" X 4 FT. X 8 FT. PLYWOOD

19 1/2"
27 7/8"
P P
P P P P P P

1/4" X 4 FT. X 8 FT. PLY OR MASONITE (8 BOTTOMS) 9 TH FROM SCRAP

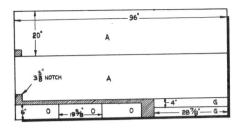

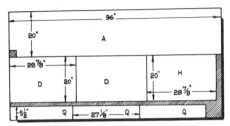

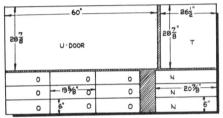

ALL THREE PANELS ARE 3/4" X 4 FT. X 8 FT. PLYWOOD

starting with the bottom one and using the spacer to position each succeeding frame. Frames can be held in place by nails driven into them through the vertical panels. Coat the edges of the frames with glue before nailing them. Another method of installing the frames and shelves would be to set them in dadoes. These would have to be cut in the vertical panels before they are erected, and dimensions controlling the width of the shelves and frames would have to be adjusted if the overall size suggested for the project is to be maintained. For example; if the dadoes are 3/8 inch deep then the width of frames and shelves must be increased by 3/4 inch. Glue and finishing nails would still be used to install them.

Make the drawers by starting with the front, cutting it to size and checking it against the opening it must fit. When one is right cut the remainder to that same size. Follow with the drawer sides—cut dadoes for the drawer bottom in sides and front. Assemble these four pieces, then add the back.

Cut the doors to provide about $\frac{1}{32}$-inch clearance on all but the hinge sides and install them with 2-inch butt hinges.

Headboard Project

Start this one by making the two

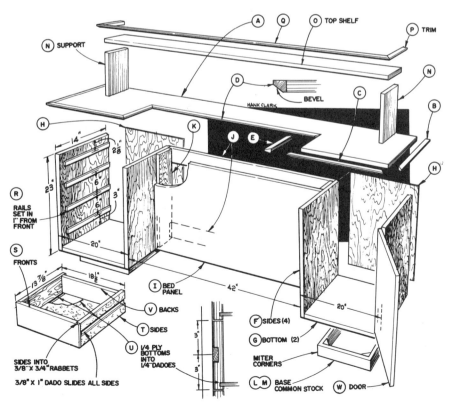

37 ◇

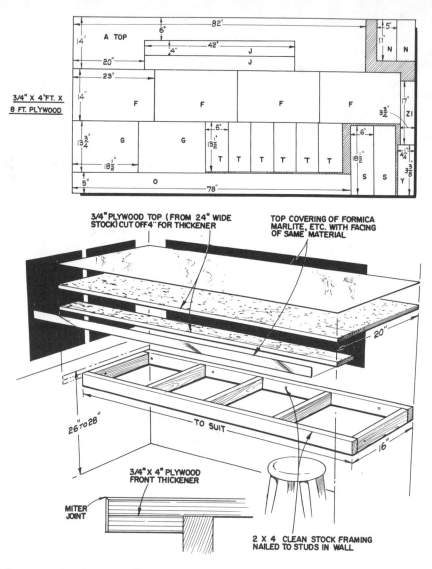

82"

A TOP

6"

J J

42"

4"

N N

5"
11"

20"

23"

F F F F

3/4" X 4'FT. X
8 FT. PLYWOOD

14"

Z1

7"

3¾"

13¾"

G G

13½"

6"

T T T T T T

6"

18½"

S S

Y

18½"

3¾"

1¾"
3⅜"

4¼"
3⅜"

5"

O

78"

3/4" PLYWOOD TOP (FROM 24" WIDE
STOCK) CUT OFF 4" FOR THICKENER

TOP COVERING OF FORMICA
MARLITE, ETC. WITH FACING
OF SAME MATERIAL

20"

26 TO 28"

TO SUIT

16"

3/4" X 4" PLYWOOD
FRONT THICKENER

MITER
JOINT

2 X 4 CLEAN STOCK FRAMING
NAILED TO STUDS IN WALL

"boxes"; one of which holds the four drawers, the other being a small cabinet. These are open at the top for the top of unit (A) will provide sufficient rigidity after it is added to the structure. It's a good idea, before assembling the drawer enclosure, to lay out carefully the positions of the drawer slides. These should be cut to exact dimensions and smoothly sanded to ride easily in the dadoes cut in the drawer sides. When you're sure they are in correct position, coat the back edge with glue and install them with small, countersunk screws. Be sure the screws are driven in far enough to be slightly under the surface of the wood so they won't interfere with drawer movement.

Assemble the box-feet (L and M) as separate units, toenailing the glue blocks

in place after coating all mating surfaces liberally with glue. Attach these to the units by nailing down into them through the base of the units.

The separator (made from parts I, J and K) is also assembled separately, then installed between the two end units with screws. It isn't necessary to use glue here.

Make the top very carefully, laying it out first on the plywood, and checking before cutting to be sure dimensions are correct.

The trim strips which edge the top of the unit and the shelf are beveled on the forward edge to gentle the appearance of the horizontal pieces. Although the bill-of-materials lists these trim strips as individual pieces, it's good practice to run this bevel on long pieces of material and to get

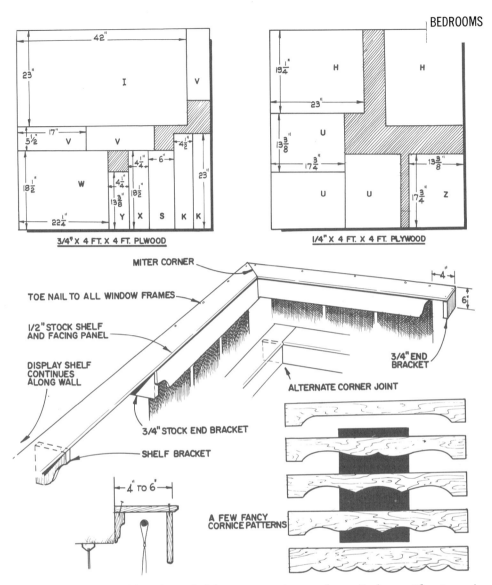

them completely shaped and sanded before sizing them. Even then, it will be more convenient to cut pieces to size as you go along, checking them on the part. Cut and fit all miters very carefully for these are most important on final appearance. Attach trim strips with glue and 2-inch finishing nails.

The two verticals which support the shelf are nailed to the shelf, but are not permanently attached to the headboard unit.

Work Counter or Desk

This is merely a 2x4 frame topped with a sheet of plywood which is in turn covered with the finishing material. If the ends and back can be rigidly attached, in this case —one end to a wall, the other to the wardrobe unit and the back to a wall—the counter can be quite long without requiring vertical supports (legs). It's best to install the frame and the plywood cover and the strip which builds up the front edge completely first. Then carefully add the Formica, using contact cement.

Cornice and Display Shelf

The cornice and shelf add the final touch to the room. Design here can definitely identify the room as being a child's or a teen-ager's, or a grown-up's. If you want to remain neutral, use a simple design. A plain cornice can be decorated (after painting) with decals. A youngster will be delighted if you decorate the cornice with overlaid, nursery-rhyme cutouts made on a jig saw and colorfully painted. • *By R. J. DeCristoforo*

THE ADDITION over the garage not only adds space but also style to your original house.

A BEDROOM OVER YOUR GARAGE -FOR A CAPE COD

by Hank Clark

One

THIS home owner wanted a garage next to the house, and so he got to work on it. But when he reached ceiling level, he saw that the next step would have to be long roof rafters up to a ridge pole. Then he realized that flat ceiling area could be a bedroom floor. The same rafters were needed, but now they would go higher over what would become a bedroom above the garage.

Since he wanted the front roof to conform to the house roof, this meant that the bedroom had to set back a bit and so a shed dormer effect was built at the rear. This adjoined the dormer that was already at the rear of the main house. Later, the window at second floor of the house was converted into a door for access to the new room.

The drawing shows much of the structure of the 2 x 4 and rafter layout. It

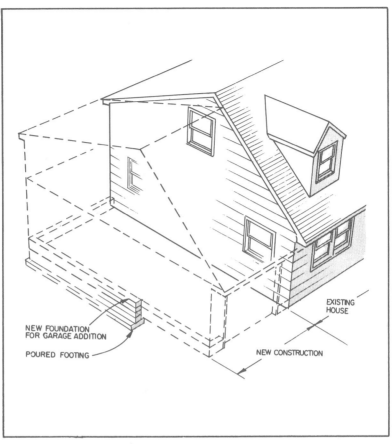

NEW FOUNDATION
FOR GARAGE ADDITION

POURED FOOTING

EXISTING
HOUSE

NEW CONSTRUCTION

THE WINDOW of the house, seen here, was converted to a door for bedroom.

FRAMING is a simple procedure on a solid foundation. Plywood sheathing follows.

WINDOWS are framed in and then the siding put on. Paint is final job.

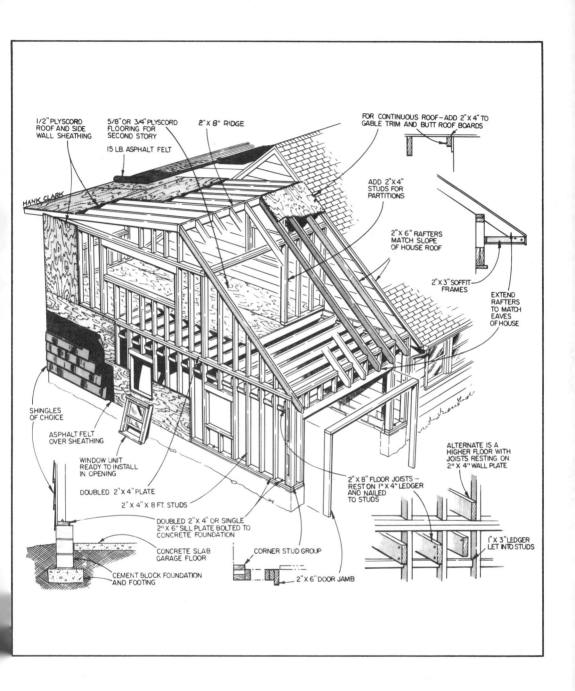

1/2" PLYSCORD ROOF AND SIDE WALL SHEATHING

5/8" OR 3/4" PLYSCORD FLOORING FOR SECOND STORY

15 LB. ASPHALT FELT

2" X 8" RIDGE

FOR CONTINUOUS ROOF—ADD 2" X 4" TO GABLE TRIM AND BUTT ROOF BOARDS

HANK CLARK

ADD 2" X 4" STUDS FOR PARTITIONS

2" X 6" RAFTERS MATCH SLOPE OF HOUSE ROOF

2" X 3" SOFFIT FRAMES

EXTEND RAFTERS TO MATCH EAVES OF HOUSE

SHINGLES OF CHOICE

ASPHALT FELT OVER SHEATHING

WINDOW UNIT READY TO INSTALL IN OPENING

DOUBLED 2" X 4" PLATE

2" X 4" X 8 FT. STUDS

DOUBLED 2" X 4" OR SINGLE 2" X 6" SILL PLATE BOLTED TO CONCRETE FOUNDATION

CONCRETE SLAB GARAGE FLOOR

CEMENT BLOCK FOUNDATION AND FOOTING

CORNER STUD GROUP

2" X 6" DOOR JAMB

2" X 8" FLOOR JOISTS – REST ON 1" X 4" LEDGER AND NAILED TO STUDS

ALTERNATE IS A HIGHER FLOOR WITH JOISTS RESTING ON 2" X 4" WALL PLATE

1" X 3" LEDGER LET INTO STUDS

all rests of course, upon a cement foundation, poured or blocked. In some areas of the country you can legally get away with post and pier support for second floors, but in major suburbia the building code requires that you have solid foundations, set below frost line.

Sheathing is usually plywood, over which you place asphalt felt, then the final shingles. You should know in advance the window sizes you'll use, so you can frame the openings to accommodate as you build. All in all, it's a simple structure for the handyman. •

43 ◊

A BEDROOM
OVER YOUR GARAGE
-FOR A SPLIT-LEVEL

Two by Hank Clark

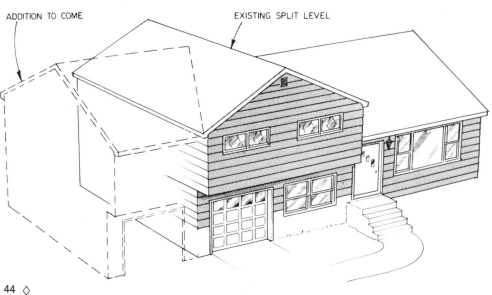

ADDITION TO COME   EXISTING SPLIT LEVEL

TWO UPSTAIRS bedrooms were this man's goal when he added a new garage next to his existing one—for his split level house.

He got them by not gabling the garage with worthless rafters, but making a flat floor overhead; then going up one more flight to make the bedrooms.

The gable went over the bedrooms, of course, and tied into the existing second floor at 90° to form another "wing" to his home. The second floor extends out to the same cantilever as the adjacent rooms.

Of course, the usual concrete footing and foundation wall must be poured or built of cement block to support half a garage wall, plus all the upstairs; though the garage door has a double header over that open span.

For the bedroom floor you may run 2"x 8" joists from the house wall out across the garage; but the front extension joists must run from the front to some 8 feet back so that they join a header. Otherwise the upstairs cannot extend outward.

Finally, the outer walls are sheathed with plywood or celotex, with siding to match the existing house siding. •

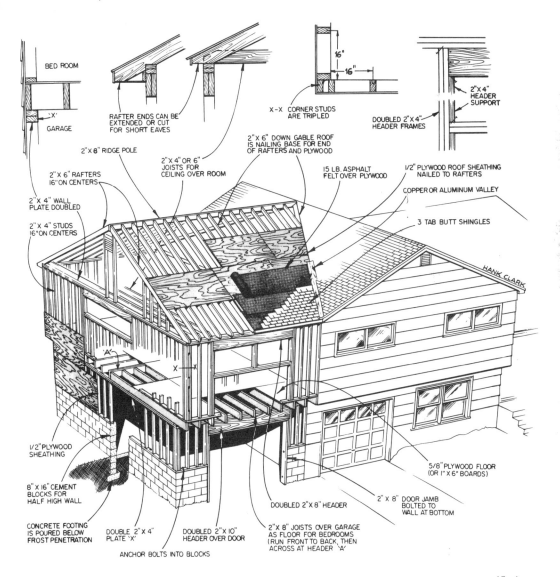

BED ROOM

'X'

GARAGE

RAFTER ENDS CAN BE EXTENDED OR CUT FOR SHORT EAVES

2" X 8" RIDGE POLE

2" X 6" RAFTERS 16" ON CENTERS

2" X 4" WALL PLATE DOUBLED

2" X 4" STUDS 16" ON CENTERS

2" X 4" OR 6" JOISTS FOR CEILING OVER ROOM

2" X 6" DOWN GABLE ROOF IS NAILING BASE FOR END OF RAFTERS AND PLYWOOD

X-X CORNER STUDS ARE TRIPLED

DOUBLED 2" X 4" HEADER FRAMES

15 LB. ASPHALT FELT OVER PLYWOOD

1/2" PLYWOOD ROOF SHEATHING NAILED TO RAFTERS

COPPER OR ALUMINUM VALLEY

3 TAB BUTT SHINGLES

2" X 4" HEADER SUPPORT

HANK CLARK

'A'

X—X

1/2" PLYWOOD SHEATHING

8" X 16" CEMENT BLOCKS FOR HALF HIGH WALL

CONCRETE FOOTING IS POURED BELOW FROST PENETRATION

DOUBLE 2" X 4" PLATE 'X'

ANCHOR BOLTS INTO BLOCKS

DOUBLED 2" X 10" HEADER OVER DOOR

DOUBLED 2" X 8" HEADER

2" X 8" JOISTS OVER GARAGE AS FLOOR FOR BEDROOMS (RUN FRONT TO BACK, THEN ACROSS AT HEADER 'A')

2" X 8" DOOR JAMB BOLTED TO WALL AT BOTTOM

5/8" PLYWOOD FLOOR (OR 1" X 6" BOARDS)

45 ◇

Bedroom Hamper

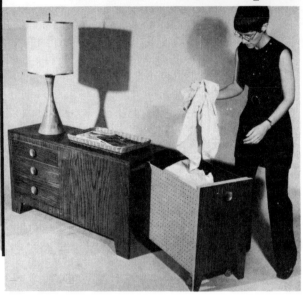

By Jackson Hand

DOUBLE utility as a chest and as a camouflaged clothes hamper earns this project a place in any bedroom—and its small materials list makes it economical and quick to build. It is proportioned to stand against a wall—or across the foot of a double bed. In style, it has the look of a long, delicate commode, but one end rolls out on casters, revealing a hamper constructed of pegboard. You can build it in the contemporary design shown here, or with minor changes in materials and shapes, make it colonial in design.

The project takes less than a sheet of ¾-in. cabinet grade plywood with your choice of veneer, about half a sheet of ½-in. fir plywood for functional parts, about the same amount of pegboard, a quarter sheet of ¼-in. fir for drawer bottoms, a few lengths of molding or wood tape, a few scraps of 1-in. pine, 3 casters and 4 drawer pulls. Construction is simple: glue and screws or nails.

We used oak-faced plywood, and stained it a medium, teak-like brown, to accentuate its naturally prominent grain. It would have looked fine, too, stained jet black. Walnut, teak, or rosewood plywood, finished with a pene-

trating finish such as deep-finish Firzite or Dupont Penetrating Wood Finish, would also look good.

If your furnishings lean toward the traditional, you might like to use pine plywood and handle the feet and edges with the standard shapes and moldings available. Pine plywood gives a good early American or colonial result when stained with a pigmented wiping stain such as Minwax Early American.

To keep the project simple and quick to build, all joints are butts, held together with screwed-and-glued cleats. Wood tape covers the edges of the plywood where they are exposed, or are hidden by ogee molding if you make the colonial design.

Put the stationary part of the hamper-chest together first, then you can be sure to size the roll-in-roll-out hamper so it operates smoothly.

Cut out the components for the chest proper. Fasten the drawer supports to the chest end and the ½-inch plywood divider, then fasten the divider to the back. Join front to the end and the end to the back. Put the top in place.

Cut and assemble the roll-out hamper. The only critical step is determining the height of the blocks on which the three casters are mounted. This distance depends on the actual height of the casters you select. Be sure the hamper rolls into its stall under the top, without too much space—or too little. Drill the holes for the casters before you glue the mounting blocks in place.

The rather novel drawer construction makes it easy to provide the ¾-in. hang-down lip required to cover the drawer dividers. To assemble these drawers, you nail-and-glue the ¼-in. bottoms to the ½-in. sides and backs. Then, the bottom fits into the ¼-in. groove in the drawer front and the sides fit into the dadoes. (You can use the conventional floating bottom method of drawer construction if your sense of craftsmanship demands it; however, with drawers of this size expansion and contraction are unlikely to be acute

enough to cause trouble with the corner joints.)

The final step in construction is to apply wood tape (or the ogee molding, as the case may be) to the exposed edges of the plywood. Some wood tapes have pressure-sensitive adhesives; others have a tough paper backing, excellent for gluing. Use contact cement—or the newest type of adhesive for such materials: double-coated tape. The ogee molding should be applied with glue and small brads, countersunk and filled.

If you use a pigmented wiping stain, you probably won't need a filler. Most contain sufficient sealer so that you get a finish with one coat of satin urethane varnish over the stain. For more protection and a nicer finish, add a second coat of varnish. Depending on the use you'll give the piece, it may be a good idea to recoat the top, at least. •

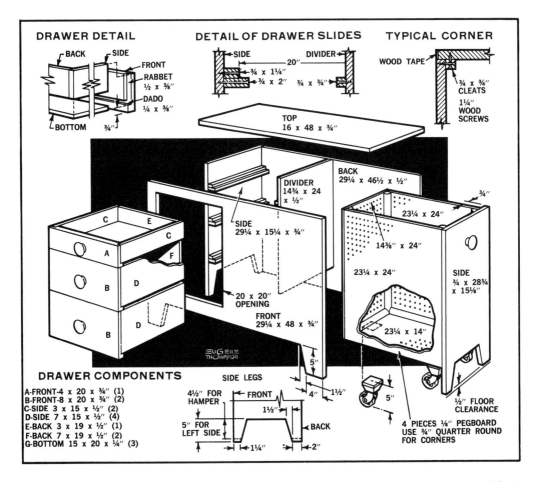

DRAWER DETAIL — BACK, SIDE, FRONT, RABBET ½ x ⅜″, DADO ¼ x ⅜″, BOTTOM ¾″

DETAIL OF DRAWER SLIDES — SIDE, 20″, DIVIDER, ¾ x 1¼″, ¾ x 2″, ¾ x ¾″

TYPICAL CORNER — WOOD TAPE, ¾ x ¾″ CLEATS, 1¼″ WOOD SCREWS

TOP 16 x 48 x ¾″

DIVIDER 14¾ x 24 x ½″

BACK 29¼ x 46½ x ½″

23¼ x 24″

SIDE 29¼ x 15¼ x ¾″

14⅜″ x 24″

23¼ x 24″

SIDE ¾ x 28¾ x 15⅛″

20 x 20″ OPENING

FRONT 29¼ x 48 x ¾″

23¼ x 14″

¾″

5″

4″   1½″   5″

½″ FLOOR CLEARANCE

4 PIECES ⅛″ PEGBOARD USE ¾″ QUARTER ROUND FOR CORNERS

EUGENE THOMPSON

DRAWER COMPONENTS

A-FRONT-4 x 20 x ¾″ (1)
B-FRONT-8 x 20 x ¾″ (2)
C-SIDE 3 x 15 x ½″ (2)
D-SIDE 7 x 15 x ½″ (4)
E-BACK 3 x 19 x ½″ (1)
F-BACK 7 x 19 x ½″ (2)
G-BOTTOM 15 x 20 x ¼″ (3)

SIDE LEGS

4½″ FOR HAMPER

5″ FOR LEFT SIDE

FRONT

1½″

1½″

BACK

1¼″   2″

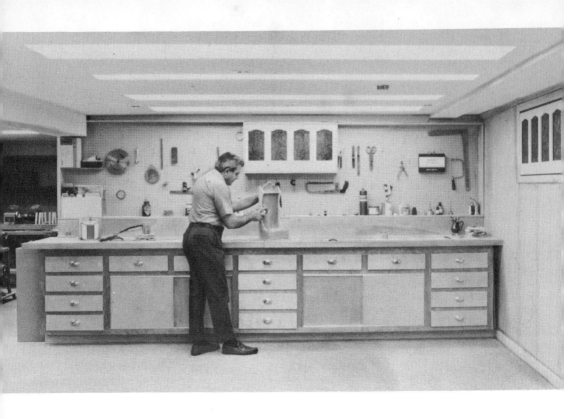

The Superbench
For Handymen With King-Size Needs

WHAT our Superbench has going for it is space . . . space galore. The top is 2 ft. wide and 14 ft. long and the base has 16 slide-out drawers and a couple of cavernous compartments. On the wall above is a big pegboard backdrop for hanging things. In sum, the bench is big enough to make any building job easier and house half a hardware store.

If Superbench should happen to be just too, too much for you there's still no problem. Construction is such that you could build only part of the bench without a major plan revision and still retain balanced good looks and usefulness. For example, you might exclude the portion of the bench from the beginning of the large compartment on the right side on. That'd leave you with a neat workbench with ten drawers, one compartment and a healthy 8 ft. of working space.

AS you secure partitions to the back, fasten plywood strips in notches with nails.

Use ¾-in. lumber-core birch plywood wherever wood is visible in the completed piece. Start construction by making the back, 43 in. wide (high) and 13 ft. long, joining two pieces of plywood with splines or dowels to get the length. To this attach partitions (eight in all) as shown in the drawing, nailing through the back to secure them. As you can see, each partition is notched at the top (¾ x 2 in.) and at the bottom (4 x 4 in.) and cleated. As you secure partitions, lay a strip of plywood in the top notches and fasten it in place. To cover the entire length, spline two strips together.

The front of the base really is just a framework for drawers and compartment doors. It is composed of 2-in.-wide plywood strips joined with splines. Nail the strips to the front edges of the partitions. Use long single strips along the top and bottom, filling in between with shorter horizontal and vertical pieces. Nail facing strips along the 4 x 4 in.

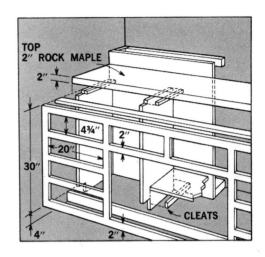

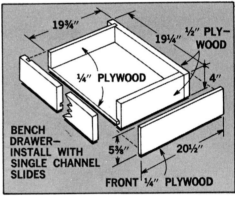

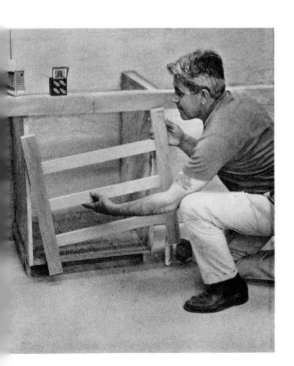

MAKE front framework in sections, then secure them to the front edges of the partitions.

notches to form the kick space. Install the drawers and the sliding doors.

Nail a 2 x 4-in. plate to the floor and a wall cleat above it (see drawing), then push the free-standing base against the plate. Secure furring strips where the pegboard will be. Cut pegboard to cover the area, then nail the material to a frame made of 5-in.-wide plywood strips. Mount the pegboard on top of the cleat and back of the base. Secure by nailing into the cleat and back and screwing through holes in the pegboard into the furring strips.

Use 2 in.-thick laminated rock-maple boards for the top. Just set them in place—they're so heavy no fastening is necessary. •

SLAT BENCH AND CABINET

By Peter Gowland

The simple design of this useful and attractive piece of
furniture makes it as easy to build as it is to look at.

RECORD STORAGE or magazine rack, even hi-fi or radio can be housed in this modern design by Don Staska. Unique slat bench lends an interesting contrast in texture to the cabinet.

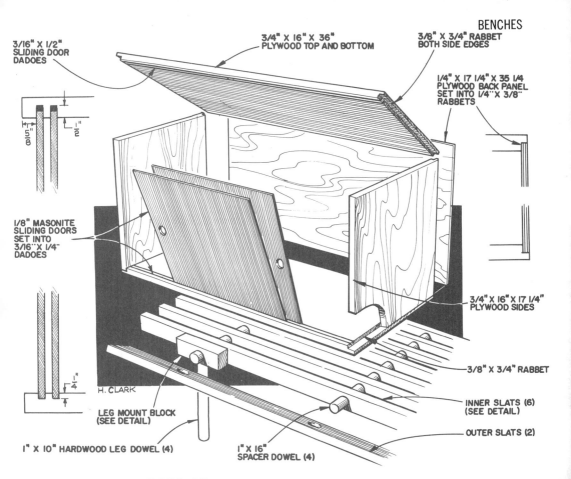

3/16" X 1/2" SLIDING DOOR DADOES

3/4" X 16" X 36" PLYWOOD TOP AND BOTTOM

3/8" X 3/4" RABBET BOTH SIDE EDGES

1/4" X 17 1/4" X 35 1/4 PLYWOOD BACK PANEL SET INTO 1/4" X 3/8" RABBETS

1/8" MASONITE SLIDING DOORS SET INTO 3/16" X 1/4" DADOES

3/4" X 16" X 17 1/4" PLYWOOD SIDES

3/8" X 3/4" RABBET

H. CLARK

LEG MOUNT BLOCK (SEE DETAIL)

INNER SLATS (6) (SEE DETAIL)

OUTER SLATS (2)

1" X 10" HARDWOOD LEG DOWEL (4)

1" X 16" SPACER DOWEL (4)

CONSTRUCTION DETAILS OF both cabinet and bench are shown above. Note simple sliding door construction in which Masonite panels fit into the grooves in top and bottom.

A PROJECT that can be easily made in the average home workshop, this bench and cabinet are made of simple components which, for the would-be home craftsman who does not have a workshop, can be obtained at most lumberyards, cut to size and milled as required; the only other tools necessary are the basic things found in most homes—some glue, a hammer, some elbow grease and adequate enthusiasm.

When completed, the bench can be stained or painted as desired; the doors can be painted a bright color for a bit of accent. Shelves or trays can be added to the cabinet to add to its usefulness. Use the cabinet for record storage or to hold magazines. •

MATERIALS LAID OUT and ready to assemble include eight 1x2 six-feet-long slats with one-inch holes drilled on 18-inch centers, beginning nine inches in from either end.

BEGIN ASSEMBLING BENCH by inserting four spacer dowels with one 2x2 spacer block located at either end of bench. Assemble additional slats over the dowels. Use remaining spacer blocks as a guide for assembling slats as shown. Hold slats in place with nails.

FINISHED BENCH is now ready for varnish, paint or stain. A good idea would be to give all pieces a coat of finishing material before assembly due to relative inaccessability of inside areas. Cut and groove all cabinet pieces as shown above. Doors are 1/8-inch Masonite, each 14 inches high, 8 inches wide. Sides, top and bottom are 3/4-inch plywood rabbeted as shown. Note dado cuts for sliding doors. Top dadoes cut deeper for assembly.

ASSEMBLE CABINET SIDES, top and bottom panels using glue and one-inch brads. Note that a square is used to properly line up side panels. Countersink nail heads, fill, sand before finishing. The 1/4-inch plywood backing is now set into rabbeted area and fastened in place.

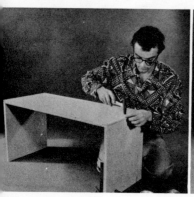

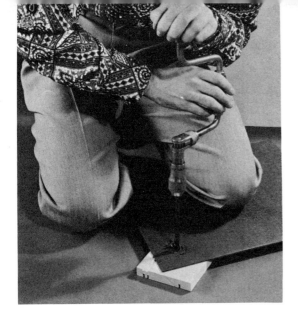

CAREFULLY DRILL ½-inch round hole in bottom corners of each sliding door for finger pulls. Use wood backing.

DADO CUTS FOR sliding doors are ½-inch deep on top piece, ¼-inch deep on bottom, permits easy assembly and removal.

FINISHED CABINET is simply set on one end of the bench and finished to suit. Cabinet, of course, can be set on either end.

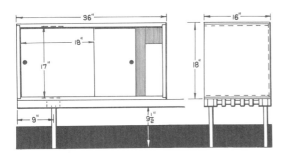

USE HARDWOOD for slats and bench construction in general for necessary strength, softer wood in this design would simply not hold up. Further construction details are shown above and at right. For a final decorative touch, paint doors a bright color to accent. Colorful toss pillows can be set on the bench to complement the doors. Bench can be used as a table to hold plants, magazines or books as desired.

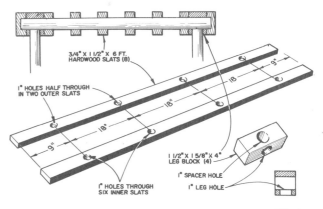

3/4" X 1 1/2" X 6 FT. HARDWOOD SLATS (8)

1" HOLES HALF THROUGH IN TWO OUTER SLATS

1 1/2" X 1 5/8" X 4" LEG BLOCK (4)

1" SPACER HOLE

1" LEG HOLE

1" HOLES THROUGH SIX INNER SLATS

BICYCLE RACK

Make this six-bike

rack without threading

a single piece of pipe!

by John Michaels

SLIP on some fittings and tighten set-screws. Outside of cutting tubing and pipe to length, that's all that's required to build this rack which holds up to six bikes—and it's a great thing to have on the premises when Junior's bike brigade comes calling.

The fittings which make assembly so easy are manufactured by the John Hosking Co., 1704 Howland Place, Cincinnati 23, Ohio, and are sold through hardware outlets. Instead of interior threads, they have setscrews housed in diamond-shaped bosses and these screws are simply turned down on the pipe or tubing. The company makes a complete line of fittings for all types of pipe and tube structures and the handyman can now do a professional job without cutting a single thread. In fact, with the adjustable elbows, tees and other fittings in the line, bending of the pipe or tubing isn't even necessary.

To make the rack, 1-inch and ¾-inch O.D. galvanized iron pipe is first cut to size with a pipe cutter. In the 1-inch piping, you'll need four 36-inch, four 12-inch and two 21½-inch lengths; in ¾-inch pipe, you'll need six 24-inch lengths. After drilling $1\frac{3}{16}$-inch holes in the horizontal center sections, spacing them as indicated on the drawing, you just work from the bottom up, slipping on fittings and tightening screws.

BASE of rack is assembled first. Piping doesn't have to be threaded for fittings.

SPACER PIPES fit into holes in the larger pipes and then the top elbows are secured.

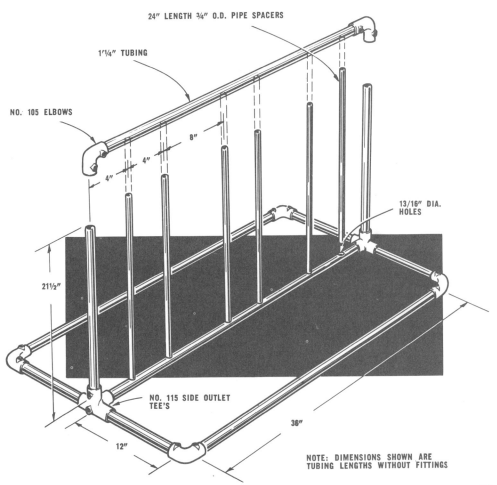

24" LENGTH ¾" O.D. PIPE SPACERS

1'1¼" TUBING

NO. 105 ELBOWS

8"

4"

4"

4"

13/16" DIA. HOLES

21½"

NO. 115 SIDE OUTLET TEE'S

36"

12"

NOTE: DIMENSIONS SHOWN ARE TUBING LENGTHS WITHOUT FITTINGS

BIRD BATH

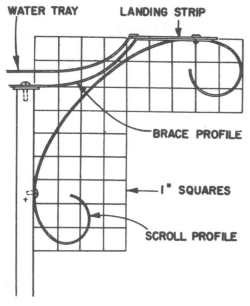

WATER TRAY   LANDING STRIP

BRACE PROFILE

1" SQUARES

SCROLL PROFILE

THE wide "landing strip" of this bird bath is an open invitation to any winged visitor to your garden. Its copper and brass construction will last indefinitely, actually improving with age.

For the water pan, turn a wood form to the final shape, then put the form and a piece of 22 ga. copper, 10-in. diameter, onto a metal or wood lathe. Complete the spinning with a shaped hardwood tool, braced against the tool post. Mutton tallow may be used as a lubricant. To finish, polish and lacquer to prevent tarnishing.—*C. A. Martin*

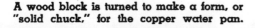

A wood block is turned to make a form, or "solid chuck," for the copper water pan.

Using a lathe, copper is spun against the form with help of a shaped hardwood tool.

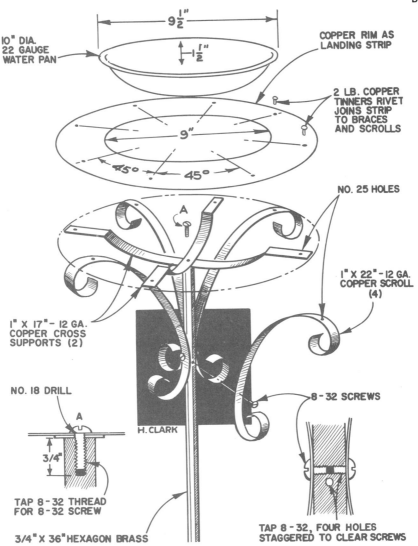

10" DIA. 22 GAUGE WATER PAN

$9\frac{1}{2}$"

$1\frac{1}{2}$"

COPPER RIM AS LANDING STRIP

2 LB. COPPER TINNERS RIVET JOINS STRIP TO BRACES AND SCROLLS

9"

45° 45°

NO. 25 HOLES

A

1" X 22" - 12 GA. COPPER SCROLL (4)

1" X 17" - 12 GA. COPPER CROSS SUPPORTS (2)

8 - 32 SCREWS

NO. 18 DRILL

A

3/4"

H. CLARK

TAP 8 - 32 THREAD FOR 8 - 32 SCREW

3/4" X 36" HEXAGON BRASS

TAP 8 - 32, FOUR HOLES STAGGERED TO CLEAR SCREWS

All copper scrollwork can easily be bent with a Metl-Former or around a cylinder.

Brass screws attach scrolls to center post, after they are riveted onto landing strip.

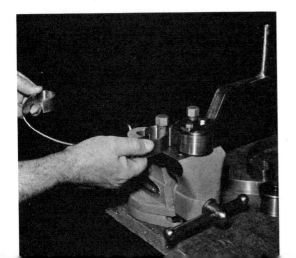

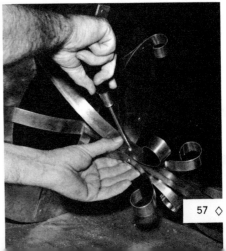

HOW TO PATCH A

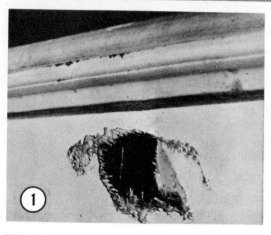

THIS fiberglass boat was punctured above the waterline when driven ashore in a storm. The damaged area measures about 6" by 3".

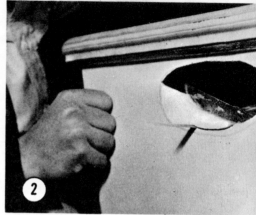

FIRST STEP is to mark entire damaged area with grease pencil, then carefully trim it out with a keyhole saw or other small saw.

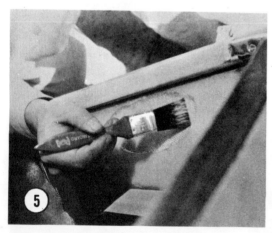

CUT three pieces of 10-oz. glass cloth, first being size of hole, others larger. Apply with resin, starting with smallest.

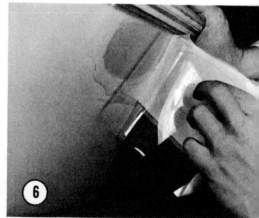

WHEN all the resin has cured, peel off the cardboard and acetate and sand down ridges of resin on outside of the hull.

ARE you still sitting around staring glumly at that hole your son managed to punch in the fiberglass runabout last summer? Cheer up! Repairing a punctured fiberglass boat isn't as difficult as you may have imagined.

The pictures on these pages show you the easy, uncomplicated procedure. And, if you're careful enough on the finishing end, no one but you (and your son) ever will know that the hull was damaged to begin with.

FIBERGLASS BOAT

BEVEL inside edges of the hole with rasp, then sand a good-size area around hole to allow for overlap of fiberglass cloth.

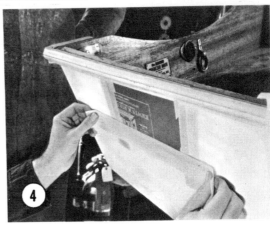

CUT pieces of cardboard and clear acetate larger than cut-out area, tape to outside of hull, back-to-back, acetate to inside.

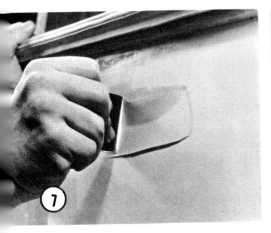

MIX a small batch of filler compound, such as Kuhl's Epotex, then apply with putty knife to newly sanded outside area.

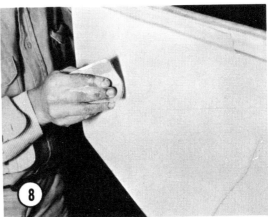

WHEN compound hardens, sand smooth, then apply coat of fiberglass primer. Finish off with two coats of good marine paint.

A word of caution: when applying the resin to the first piece of cloth in the hole area, don't try to put too much around the edges. The fiberglass cloth should be wet through entirely with the resin but too much in this area will result in much of it seeping between the acetate and hull to harden on the outside. Then you'll be sanding forever to get a smooth surface. Incidentally, the sanding of resin and cloth combined will be done better by machine. •

Top Off Your Boat

Even at top speed of 25 mph, canvas is snug, doesn't flap.

SMALL boat owners who want relief from a blistering sun or some measure of shelter in a light shower can make this canvas top for less than $15. The only materials needed are some 12-oz. canvas, two 10-ft. lengths of aluminum tubing or electrical conduit, some aluminum clothesline and odds and ends of hardware.

The frames are bent at the width of

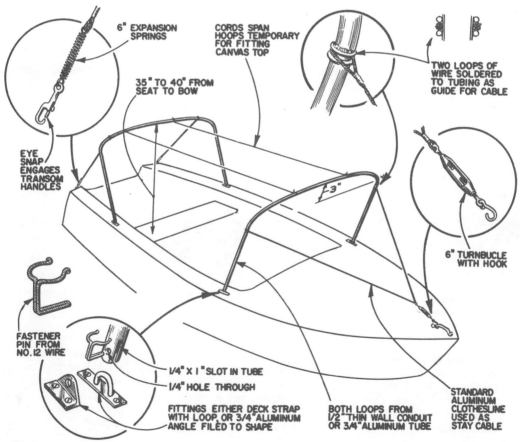

6" EXPANSION SPRINGS

CORDS SPAN HOOPS TEMPORARY FOR FITTING CANVAS TOP

TWO LOOPS OF WIRE SOLDERED TO TUBING AS GUIDE FOR CABLE

35" TO 40" FROM SEAT TO BOW

EYE SNAP ENGAGES TRANSOM HANDLES

3"

6" TURNBUCLE WITH HOOK

FASTENER PIN FROM NO. 12 WIRE

1/4" X 1" SLOT IN TUBE

1/4" HOLE THROUGH

FITTINGS EITHER DECK STRAP WITH LOOP OR 3/4" ALUMINUM ANGLE FILED TO SHAPE

BOTH LOOPS FROM 1/2" THIN WALL CONDUIT OR 3/4" ALUMINUM TUBE

STANDARD ALUMINUM CLOTHESLINE USED AS STAY CABLE

Use full-size template for conduit bending; use sand if no bending tool is available.

57-146

Canvas is hemmed at both ends, then slipped onto the conduit. Note slight bow across top.

To allow cable to move on conduit, solder two washers on conduit with cable between.

Brackets made from aluminum angles hold conduits. Bend fasteners from No. 12 wire.

the boat and it's best to do the job on a bending tool. If you don't have one yourself, the dealer who sells the conduit probably has. Leave the conduit long at both sides, then position each frame on the boat and cut off the ends at the proper length for passenger comfort and motor access.

Tie the two frames together on the boat and determine the right slant for the best appearance. When they're in the right position, the required lengths of cable and canvas can be measured.

When the canvas is cut to size, a waterproofing agent is applied. Then the sides are hemmed and 2-in. looped hems are made at the ends so that the conduit slips through easily.

A word of caution: Don't take chances with any kind of top on a small boat if you intend to use it on open water that can really rough up. When the weather looks as if it will go bad, best take the top down. Waves lifting the boat and wind under the canvas will work to flip you over. If rain is accompanied by wind and waves, the canvas offers no shelter anyway. •

Photos courtesy Petit Paint Co.

It is easy to scrape an old surface after paint remover has caused it to bubble up.

Plastic composition wood can fill this hole. Sand the area first and wipe away all dirt.

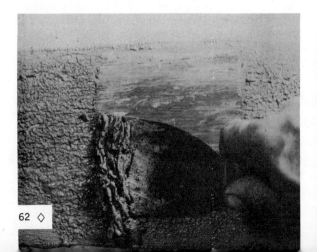

Hull Repair

By John Kingdon

THE man who intends to fit out and paint his own boat in the spring must have the patience of a Missouri farmer who owns a stubborn mule. Fifty per cent of his efforts will be put forth in scrubbing, patching and sanding before the paint brush comes into play. And, as if this were not enough, the rest of his activity will be punctuated with eight to 48-hour waiting periods between coats of paint.

All this is not meant to sour you on painting, but merely to point up the basic fact that a first-rate paint job can be achieved only if you get an early start and proceed slowly.

Actually, fitting out need not be a chore. If the skipper, the first mate and all the little mates pitch into the work, it can be satisfying family fun. And when the craft slides into the water, all concerned will feel happy because of a good job well done.

Also, don't ignore your friends when making up your work gang. They'll expect to be invited aboard during the summer, so there's no reason why they shouldn't help out in the spring.

For best maintenance, you should paint your boat each year. If the previous paint job was a good one, this yearly maintenance chore will be relatively simple. But if last year's paint was haphazardly applied or if the finish is checked and cracking, resign yourself to a major reconditioning.

The first thing to do is to remove all hardware and other detachable items such as seats, locker doors, hatch covers and the like. Next, using a mild detergent, hot water and a fairly stiff brush, scrub off dirt, oil, grease and algae; then hose the boat off and let it dry.

Reconditioning

When everything's dry, inspect the hull to decide whether or not it needs a major refinishing or just repainting. If the finish is in good shape, all that remains is to sand the hull lightly and to apply a coat or two of paint and/or varnish. But if the surface is afflicted with large checked or cracked areas, the boat will have to be refinished completely, which means removing all the old paint down to the bare wood and starting from scratch.

For a major reconditioning, here are the steps to follow:

1. Soften the old paint. You can use a paste-type paint remover, blowtorch, infra-red lamp or electric flatiron.

If paint remover is employed, two applications may be needed to cut through the many layers of old paint. After scraping the paint and remover off, wash down the wood with alcohol or turpentine to take off wax left by the remover.

Spread plastic dough generously in crevices (left) with wide-bladed knife. For shallow marks (center), apply a plastic surfacer. Large, marked areas (right) call for glazing compound.

When sanding by hand, abrasive will work better if a 2x3-in. wooden block is used.

To make a new seam, use a spike to rake out old seam filler and caulking cotton.

The blowtorch is quick but dangerous. If you have never handled one before, take a lesson in its use from an experienced operator: never bring it into play without having a fire extinguisher handy. Above all, don't ever use paint remover and then follow up immediately with a blowtorch. Some paint removers are so highly flammable that a surface treated with one of them will burst into flame if a blowtorch is brought to bear on it.

The infra-red lamp is slower but safer. This lamp or bulb is the type employed to alleviate stiff muscles. It can be used in any portable electric fixture that has a reflector. Hold the lamp about one inch from the surface until blisters form, then move it along slowly and follow it with a scraper.

The electric flatiron is the slowest but perhaps the most easily come by of all the paint softeners. To use, simply "iron" the paint until the surface is soft. Work but a small area at a time.

2. Remove the soft paint. Various kinds of scrapers are available. Of these, the most useful is the scraping knife, which looks like a broad-bladed putty knife. Also needed are a cabinet scraper, which has a working edge at each end, and a triangular scraper with a wooden handle. Care must be taken when using the latter to avoid digging into the wood with the points. To remove stubborn traces of paint and to clean out cracks, employ a stiff wire brush.

For raking out old seam compound sharpen and bend over the tang of an old flat file. (The tang is the slender projecting shank that fits into the wooden handle.) Bend the tang by heating it to a cherry red and hammer-ing it to quarter-circle shape over a steel rod held in a vise. When the tang is cool, file or grind it to a chisel point. Then reharden it by heating it again to a cherry red and plunging it in cold water.

3. If any hull repairs are needed, now's the time for them to be done. If you are not an expert woodworker, it's best to leave major jobs to the boatyard or someone experienced in such work. Never try to do work on your craft which is beyond your honest capacity. Replacing the deck or putting in new planks, for example, involves special knowledge and hours of really tough, backbreaking labor. They are tasks for the professional.

But there are some repairs that are easily made. As an example, look at a metal rowlock socket. Probably you never gave it a thought, but this insignificant fitting is constantly exposed. Water seeps in at the joint between it and the wood in which it is set and stays there. In time the wood rots and one day, when you put a little extra pep into a stroke, the fastenings let go, causing the entire socket to give way. Unless you're good at sculling, you may find yourself in a bad spot. How much simpler it would have been to install new fastenings or new wood beforehand.

And what holds true for the rowlock socket is also valid for such common deck fitting as chocks, cleats and bitts. Often, all that's needed to restore one of these fittings to first-class condition is to replace the wood screws with through bolts, washers and nuts.

Perhaps such things as a rub rail, a seat or a false stem may need replacing. When removing one of these parts, it

Roll new cotton into a seam with a caulking wheel or tap it in with a caulking iron.

Finish topside seams with generous amount of seam compound; let dry 24 to 28 hours.

is usually possible to cut off stubborn nails by shoving a hacksaw blade (without its frame) into the joint and sawing back and forth. This is preferable to ripping the part off and possibly damaging sound members in the process.

Or if the part is screwed in place, don't mangle the screw with a screwdriver. Instead, use a brace with a screwdriver bit, bearing down on the handle and giving the crank short, sharp jabs. Much greater force can be applied with the brace than with a screwdriver, and, since the blade is firmly held in the slot, it can't jump out.

The old part can be used as a pattern when laying out its replacement. When installing the new part, use marine glue or paint to coat all surfaces that will be hidden. If new screws go in hard, rub them with beeswax or paraffin. Don't used soap, it contains ingredients that will attack the metal.

4. Smooth the hull down. If it is planked with conventional wood, merely sand it. If it is planked with fir plywood, apply a coat of sealer such as Firzite and let it dry before doing any sanding. Never attempt to sand bare plywood; you'll only cut into the soft wood, accentuating the wild grain. Don't use a clear sealer on plywood that is to be painted. Instead, get the white type which contains a pigment that makes it a first coat of paint as well as a sealer.

There are five abrasive minerals commonly used for sandpaper. Three—flint, garnet and emery—are natural minerals; the other two—aluminum oxide and silicon carbide—are synthetics. The synthetics are much the stronger and longer-lasting.

Flint is the most generally used abrasive mineral. It is, however, the softest and has the shortest cutting life.

Garnet is reddish-brown in color and produces satisfactory results with a minimum of labor.

Emery is a black mineral with rounded, granular surfaces. Although it is a relatively dull cutting agent, it is an excellent abrasive for removing rust and corrosion from metal surfaces.

Aluminum oxide is gray-brown in color. It makes an excellent sandpaper for both metal and wood.

Silicon carbide is shiny black. It is the hardest and sharpest of all the sandpaper abrasives.

The most suitable of these for your purpose is either garnet or aluminum oxide. For rough sanding, use No. 1-50. For removing small imperfections and light scratches, employ No. 1/0 (80). And for a fine surface, finish up with No. 3/0 (100).

Sanding by hand is tiring. For this reason, the use of an electric sander is advised. If you don't have one, it can probably be rented from a nearby hardware store. Four kinds are manufactured: reciprocating (or vibrating), orbital, belt and disk. The last two are the fastest, but must be used with care by the amateur if he is to avoid scarring the surface by sanding too long in one spot.

5. Brush on a coat of sealer, let it dry, then sand it down.

6. Fill all dents and gashes with plastic composition wood or one of the other similar compounds on the market. Also putty all nail and screw holes and, if your boat is the type that requires it, apply seam compound. Don't apply any of these compounds before putting on the first coat of sealer. If you do, the

oils in the compounds may be so thoroughly absorbed by the wood that the compounds will dry and fall out.

Some conventionally planked boats require caulking cotton in their seams as well as seam compound. To find out whether or not such caulking is in good shape, pull out a little. If it looks black, the fibers are probably rotten and should be replaced. Either the tang of an old file (as previously described) or a putty knife can be used to dig it out.

Before putting in the new caulking flow paint into the seam to make the cotton stick better. Don't hammer the caulking in as if you were caulking a canal boat. The planking of the average small boat is too thin to be beaten with a caulking mallet. Besides, all that's needed, even in the most wide-open seams, is a thin strand of cotton. When the boat is put into the water, the wood will swell and take up the slack.

So instead of pounding in masses of caulking material, merely roll the strand of cotton into place. The tool to use is called a caulking wheel. If you can't get one, you can use a putty knife to push the cotton into the seams.

To leave room for the seam compound, keep the caulking a little below the surface. When adding the compound, finish off the seam so that it is slightly hollow. When the wood swells, this will level up.

7. Brush on another coat of sealer, let it dry, then sand just enough to take off the fuzz. For sanding here and between other coats, worn sandpaper is ideal.

8. Brush on a coat of marine undercoater and, after allowing it to dry thoroughly, sand vigorously, but not so vigorously that you get down to the wood. For a super-smooth finish, apply another coat of the undercoater. If you're going to paint your craft some color other than white, it's wise to tint this second undercoat in the desired color. Sand this coat just hard enough to provide a "tooth" to hold the finish paint.

9. Finish with two coats of marine paint, allowing the first to dry and sanding lightly before applying the second. Brush the paint in well. Two thin coats are much better than one thick one. More than two coats, on the other hand, can be bad because too many coats may get so heavy that they will break down under their own weight. This is espe-

cially important on canvas surfaces. Thick paint makes canvas crack, and once a crack starts there is no way of getting rid of it except to put down new canvas, which is a major job.

To estimate the paint remover, paint and varnish required (in gallons per coat), use the following formulas:

Paint Remover. One gallon will soften 200 square ft.

For Topsides. Multiply the length of the boat by the freeboard at the highest point and then by 1.5. Divide by 400.

For Bottoms. Multiply the length of the boat on the water line by the draft and then by 3.5. Divide by 400.

For Decks. Multiply the length of the boat by the beam and then by .75. Deduct the areas of all deck openings and cabins and then divide by 400.

For Housetops. Multiply the length by the width and divide by 400.

For Spars. Multiply the length of each by its greatest diameter (in feet or fractions thereof) and then multiply the result by 2.5 and divide by 400.

Your labor is now done. Don't, however, put the boat into the water and immediately go tearing off. Allow her several days after launching to swell up properly. Otherwise some of your carefully placed caulking and seam compound may work loose, causing a leak that can last all summer. Or the dry wood may work back and forth so much around the fastenings that the fastening holes will be forced into oval shapes, which means that even when the wood does swell the fastenings will be loose.

An alternate method of swelling the wood is to run a hose in your boat a few days before launching. At first the water will probably run out through the seams just about as fast as it comes in, but the boat will slowly start to swell up. Inside of 24 hours, she should be fairly tight. And by the time you are ready to launch, your troubles will be over.

Painting Tips

Know what materials you need for each job and make sure you have them on hand.

During the long spring evenings or on rainy days, when you cannot work on the boat, plan to do some small jobs—such as varnishing hatches, spars, furniture, etc.—at home.

To save time in cleaning up dripping

paint and retouching, always start at the top and work down. This means that if your boat is rightside up, you should finish the gunwales first and the bottom last; if the boat is upside down, you should finish the bottom first and the gunwales last.

Paint backward, working from a dry section into the wet paint of a previously coated area.

Brush vigorously to spread the paint evenly and eliminate all bubbles.

Work with strong, steady strokes.

Do not constantly rebrush a coated area.

Paint with the grain.

Paint on a dry, calm day only. Avoid windy weather and its resulting dust.

The ideal temperature for painting is between 60° and 85°. Don't paint when the weather is excessively hot. The hot sun may induce such rapid evaporation of some of the solvents that a skin will be formed on the surface with the remaining solvent imprisoned under it. This will inevitably cause "gas blistering." If you *must* paint in extremely hot weather, you can partially guard against this rapid evaporation by always working on the shady side, away from sun.

Start early in the day and quit early enough so the paint can begin to set before the evening dew forms.

It pays to use only good marine paint. Choose a well-known brand and then carefully follow the manufacturer's recommendations (printed on the label affixed to the can). Use only the thinner recommended by the manufacturer. And never mix the paints or varnishes of different manufacturers; their formulas may clash.

Stir the paint thoroughly before each application to mix the pigment with the liquid portion. The proper way to do this is to pour part of the liquid into another can and then to stir the pigment up from the bottom into the remaining liquid. When the mixture becomes absolutely smooth, stir in the extra liquid and then pour everything from one can to the other several times. If the paint has been opened and used before, a skin will have formed over it. All traces of this should be removed by straining the paint through cheesecloth.

Don't shake varnish or enamel. Doing so creates air bubbles that are hard to brush out. •

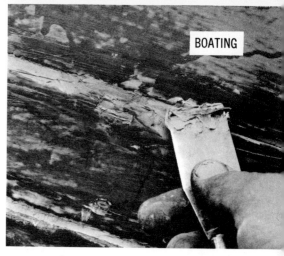

Use toxic seam cement under anti-fouling bottom paints. It repels marine organisms.

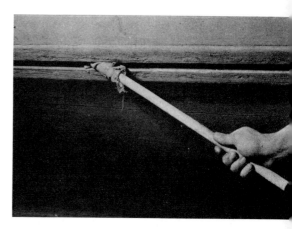

Using cloth tacked on a stick, coat centerboard trunk interior with anti-fouling paint.

Brush out paint vigorously; spread evenly. Two thin coats are better than one thick one.

Race Your Sailboat

Sailing close-hauled in a spanking breeze is enjoyment in itself, but the ultimate in satisfaction comes from racing against another craft.

By Tom Griberg

BESIDES a fleet of boats manned by enthusiastic crews, three things are required to stage a sailboat race: first, a means of signalling the start; second, a means of marking the course; and third, a set of clearly understood rules to govern the boats.

A gun shot has long been accepted as the signal for the start of a race. For this purpose, a noisy little cannon can easily be constructed from an old single-shot shotgun.

Remove and discard the stock, forearm and trigger guard and cut the barrel to a length of 11 inches. Then braze a ¼-in. nut to the bottom of the breech 2½ in. ahead of the fitting which

on the ends for cotter pins and pushed through the hole in the tailstock. The cast iron wheels are 8 in. in diameter and may be obtained at a farm implement supply store. Short pieces of ½-in. tubing are cut to fit over the axle between the wheels and the tailstock. Rubber tires are made from lengths of hose and can be held in place by threading a piece of screen door spring through the hose. The spring is cut slightly shorter than the circumference of the wheel.

Blank shotgun shells should be used in the cannon. Three shots are generally fired to start a race. We find that a five-minute warning gun followed by a one-minute warning gun and finally, the starting gun, works out very well.

To construct an efficient marker, first fasten two ¾x3x36-in. pieces of scrap lumber together in the center with a simple cross lap joint. Over the joint nail a 9x9-in. square of ¾-in. wood. This piece serves to strengthen the joint and also to give greater support to the 12-in. piece of ½-in. wall conduit which holds the flagstaff. The conduit should be forced into a drive fit hole which is drilled at center of the cross. Pinch the bottom end of conduit together so flagstaff will not slip all the way through.

Slip the ends of the cross arms through the handles of four one-gallon varnish cans. Fasten them in place with ¾-in. roundhead screws. In the center of the cross, on the underside, install a large screweye for the anchor line. Since the varnish cans will rust if not protected, give the entire construction several coats of bright-colored enamel. For flags, hem 18-in. squares of red or yellow cloth and attach them to 36-in. lengths of ½-in. dowel with copper tacks.

Lay out a race course and anchor a marker at each turn. The length of the course is optional and while a triangular course is desirable, it is not mandatory. If possible, make the first leg of the course such that the boats can be sailed close-hauled since this makes the boats easier to control at the starting line. If a series of races are planned, the markers can be left out, provided they do not interfere with navigation. Just before race, the flags can be inserted in the conduit holders.

was originally used in screwing the barrel to the forearm. Next, secure a pair of 2-in. bolts to fit the threads on these fittings. Finally, drill a small hole through the end of the trigger to take a stout cord which will serve as a lanyard.

From 2-in. oak or maple, bandsaw a tailstock as shown in the drawing and bore the required holes. Note that the end of the tailstock is hollowed out and filled with lead so that the gun will not be nose heavy. The top end should also be hollowed out to fit the underside of the breech. Then the shotgun is bolted to the tailstock.

The ½-in. diameter axle is cut from a 9-in. length of cold rolled steel, drilled

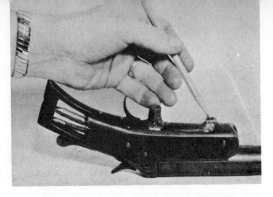

Nut brazed to underside of breech takes one of two bolts which secure tailstock.

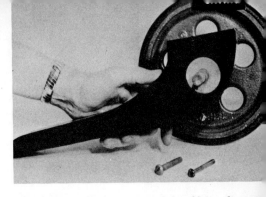

Hardwood tailstock is bored for ½-in. dia. axle made from 9-in. length of steel rod.

Shotgun and tailstock assembly is fitted on axle. Tailstock is weighted with lead.

The completed cannon. Blank shells make a loud report easily heard in all the boats.

Rules are necessary in sailboat racing, as in any sport, to give everybody an equal chance to win. However, in the case of sailboat racing, rules are even more necessary for the safety of the boats and crews. Five important rules which can be used for the governing of an enjoyable series of races are illustrated in the diagrams. Drawing 1 shows two boats converging on opposite tacks. The boat on starboard tack (wind over starboard rail with boom to port) has the right of way. Boat B on port tack must give way to boat A on starboard tack.

When converging courses on the same tack (Drawing 2) the windward boat must keep clear. Boat B to windward must give way to boat A to leeward.

When on parallel courses on the same tack (Drawing 3) the overtaking boat B must give way to the overtaken boat A.

When making a turn, an overtaking boat may demand buoy room provided he has established an overlap on the overtaken boat (Drawing 4). Boat B must give boat A room to make the turn. This rule does not apply at the starting line.

A boat crossing the starting line ahead of the starting gun (Drawing 5) must turn and recross the line. During this time he must give way to all other boats. Boat B is at fault and must turn back.

If more complete rules are desired they may be obtained for a small fee from the North American Yacht Racing Union, 37 West 44th Street, New York City, N. Y.

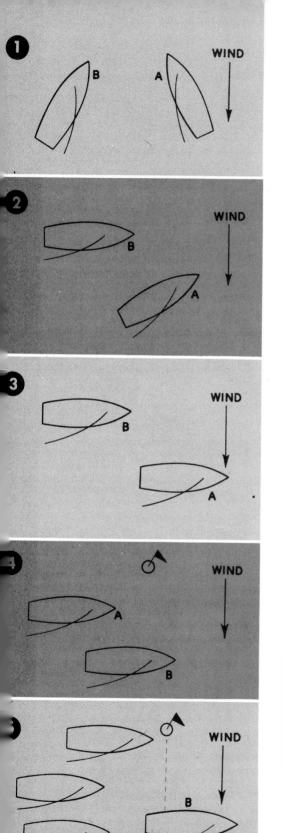

1   B   A   WIND

2   B   A   WIND

3   B   A   WIND

4   A   B   WIND

5   B   WIND

Cross pieces are simply slid under handles of cans and fastened in place with screws.

Inexpensive course marker is easily built from one-gallon cans, lumber and conduit.

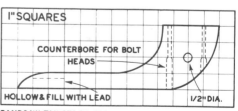

1" SQUARES

COUNTERBORE FOR BOLT HEADS

HOLLOW & FILL WITH LEAD   1/2" DIA.

BANDSAW TAILSTOCK FROM 2" OAK OR MAPLE

How To Sail

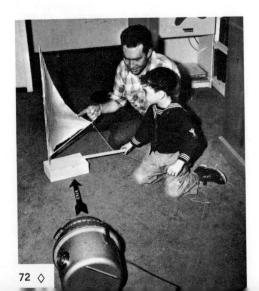

A living room trainer helps teach you how to handle your sailboat.

By Mike Drucker*

SAILING is by no means difficult and the fundamentals can be learned by the average person in a matter of hours. An obvious question arises at this point. "Can we learn to sail from a written text?" In most cases the answer is "No!" Generally nothing more can be gleaned from an article of this type than a knowledge of how it should be done.

An electric fan or the blower on a vacuum cleaner provides wind for practicing with cigar box boat.

*Director, Cap'n Mike's Sailing School, Jamaica Bay, N. Y.

The easiest way to begin to sail is on a reach. Keep the wind coming over the side of boat at about 90° from the center line. Pennant or smoke from stack can be used as wind indicator. Note direction.

In order to sail back over same line—or reach—turn boat by pushing the tiller toward boom. Draw sail in as boom swings in. When on new course let sail assume same angle as on other course.

By sailing a zig-zag course into the wind we are able to make headway in that direction. To change your tack (turn), push the tiller toward the boom. Handle on cigar box boat acts same as tiller on sailboat.

73 ◊

Musts before sailing: oars or paddles, life jacket, anchor, bailer, hat, sun glasses, and a good lunch.

However, I am attempting to do more than just that. By constructing a simple cigar box trainer and utilizing it in conjunction with an electric fan, the action of the wind on the sail can be studied at first hand. The tiller or rudder control on the trainer will act exactly as it would on a sail boat. You will be amazed at the ground you can cover without ever having cast off a mooring. A nautical purist will cringe at my obvious omission of nautical language. The use of nautical terminology in an article written for the benefit of the would-be sailor, will only add to his confusion. An individual interested in sailing will, once he has gotten his "sea legs," quickly enough acquire a nautical vocabulary, but let us get him sailing first.

The maneuvers are described in numbered sequence so they may be followed and referred to, with ease.

YOUR FIRST BOAT

If the question were put to a dozen sail boat skippers, as to their recommendations for the ideal beginner's boat, you will probably receive twelve different answers, each one using his own early experience as a basis for his choice. Therefore, I maintain that the best boat for a beginner is any sailboat he can beg, borrow or rent. Of course, it would be unwise for him to try to learn to sail on a 75-ft. schooner. Therefore, the only limitation I place is that it be a single-masted vessel of such size that an individual can handle it easily alone. The sailboat should have a fixed

counterweight in its bottom (a keel) or one with a pivoted steel plate called the centerboard. The centerboard and keel serve to prevent the boat from drifting sideways. For simplicity of description, I will assume that the boat being used is similar to the one used in the demonstration photos; that is, a single-sailed dinghy. Any additional sails will only increase the confusion. Once the basic principles are mastered, there is no problem in adapting the use of the additional jib sail. The vessel depicted in the photographs is Midge constructed from plans (No. 927) published in MECHANIX ILLUSTRATED. It is a 7½-ft. flat bottomed pram, with 27 sq. ft. of sail and a dagger type centerboard.

Before getting under way there are certain precautions that must be taken These rules should apply for the balance of your sailing career.

1. Never enter the boat without having on board an approved life jacket.

2. Do not take passengers until you are proficient in sailing.

3. Determine as best you can the weather conditions for the day and continue to observe them for the balance of the day.

4. Always have aboard a secondary means of propulsion; either oars, paddles or a small horsepower outboard motor. While in some quarters this is considered heresy, it nevertheless can save a lot of hard work for the beginner.

5. A suitable pump or bailer should be kept on board.

6. Never tie down the rope used to control the sail. Hold it in your hand at all times.

7. Face the boom when steering.

As far as clothing is concerned, I recommend a hat as a must and the balance depends on your morals, your pocketbook or your social standing.

It can safely be assumed that the person from whom the boat was commandeered will instruct the beginner in the proper method of raising sails for that particular boat.

We can now proceed to the actual mechanics of "making the boat go."

INSTRUCTIONS PRIOR TO CASTING OFF

Before casting off your first mooring, it is necessary to acquire the "feel" of the boat. By this I mean, getting to know its limits of stability, the sensitive or sluggish action of the rudder, etc. All this can be done while still safely tied to the mooring. Proceed as follows:

1. Lower the centerboard and keep it down while you are learning.

When dead into wind, sail will shake violently. Shift weight to other side and boat will continue to swing. On new course now, draw in boom close to centerline, then set at an angle of 45° to direction of wind.

When sailing downwind, keep the wind over the shoulder which is away from the boom. Tack downwind by bringing the sail in over center of boat, allowing wind on both sides as in tacking, only from rear.

Now swing the boat to the opposite side, being careful to bring the wind over the shoulder once more. Permit the sail to swing over to the new side. To get full power from wind, set the sail at about 90° angle.

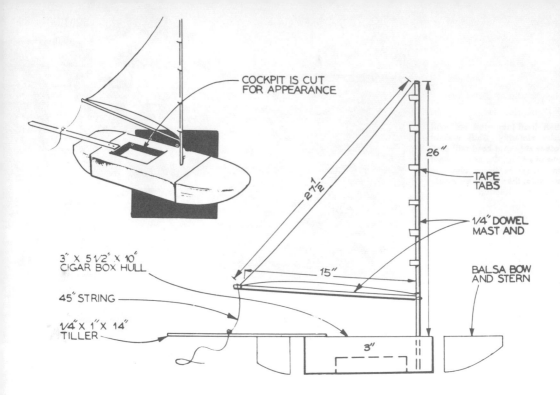

COCKPIT IS CUT
FOR APPEARANCE

26"

TAPE
TABS

1/4" DOWEL
MAST AND

BALSA BOW
AND STERN

2'7 1/2"

15"

3" X 5 1/2" X 10"
CIGAR BOX HULL

45" STRING

1/4" X 1" X 14"
TILLER

3"

2. Take your position at the tiller.

3. Bring the sail over the center of the boat and hold it there.

4. Gradually push the tiller away from you, then with force pull it towards you. This will swing the boat to one side. The wind will then strike the sail and impart a forward motion to the boat.

5. Permit the boat to sail until it has reached the limits of the anchor line.

6. Then release the sail and the tiller and permit the boat to settle back to its previous position at the end of the mooring line.

7. Repeat this until you feel more relaxed about handling the boat and until a measure of control is achieved.

Assuming that you have mastered the above, let us now actually get under way.

By simply casting off his mooring and assuming that his boat will start sailing, the beginner runs the danger of permitting his boat to collide with other moored boats. Therefore, I recommend that you row the boat to a clear area, drop the anchor, then proceed to set your sails. Once this is done, haul in the anchor and get under way. If while hauling in the anchor, you do drift back, you will then have plenty of sea room.

I recommend that all the following maneuvers be practiced with the home trainer so that you will have a good mental picture of the procedure. When using the trainer in executing a change of direction, do not

simply swing it around, but try to impart a forward motion so that a more accurate demonstration will be achieved.

SAILING ON A REACH

One of the simplest and most delightful ways of sailing is known as "a reach." When sailing in this manner, the vessel is able to sail from one point to another and return with no complicated maneuvering. A vessel is considered to be sailing on a reach when the wind is coming directly from the side of the boat. The wind indicator, a flag or a bit of ribbon in the rigging, would be pointed 90° from the center line of the boat.

1. Let us assume that we have cast off our mooring with the wind coming over the left hand side of the boat.

2. Our objective is to sail a distance away, and then to turn around and come back to the original starting point. It is always a good idea to pick an object on the shore to steer by. Proceed along with the boom tip about two feet away from the rear corner of the boat. When we have reached the point where it becomes necessary to turn the boat, push the tiller firmly to the side of the boat upon which the boom is located. Do not jam the tiller over because the boat will then lose considerable speed.

3. As the boat swings gradually around to the left, steadily haul in on the sail. Permit the boat to swing until it is headed back

to the original starting point. The wind is now coming from the right-hand side of the boat. A hard and fast rule to follow, whenever it becomes necessary to turn a boat completely around, is to push the tiller toward whatever side the boom is on. That rule will be demonstrated several times during the course of our cruise.

SAILING INTO THE WIND

Continue sailing on a reach until you have achieved complete control in making turns. This will prepare us for the next step which is the always interesting technique of sailing the boat in the direction from which the wind is blowing; that is, sailing into the wind.

It is a physical impossibility for a boat to sail directly into the wind. However, by sailing at an angle to the wind and permitting the wind to strike our sails a glancing blow, we can impart a forward motion to the boat. The procedure involves a series of zig-zag courses during which time we are able to sail approximately 45° into the wind.

Let us return to either our home trainer or our boat afloat. Assuming that during the course of our cruise and while on a reach, we decide that we would like to sail to an object which is located directly into the wind.

1. The wind while sailing on a reach is striking us directly over our left-hand side. Our boom is located on the right-hand side of the boat.

2. Following the golden rule in changing direction, we push the tiller to the boom.

3. The boat continues swinging in a windward direction until it is approximately 45° into the wind.

4. Haul the boom in to a point where the boom tip is just inside of the right hand edge of the boat.

5. Trim the sail in until all sail flapping stops.

6. Pick an object ashore as a steering guide. Continue sailing along this tack until the point we wish to reach appears to be at right angles to our course.

7. Now prepare for the next zig-zag leg which will bring us closer to our objective. Execute the maneuver for turning, i. e., ease the tiller in the direction of the boom while simultaneously drawing in the boom over the center line of the boat. The boat will then swing around. For an instant the boat will be pointed directly into the wind with the sails shaking violently. As the boat continues to swing around, the wind will strike the sail more fully and the boat will begin to gather headway. Once again sail

on a 45° course into the wind, holding the sail rope firmly in hand.

When sailing close into the wind, a boat will achieve its greatest angle of heel. The method used to avoid a capsize due to a sudden puff is to release the strain on the sail by permitting it to swing out freely, thus spilling the wind. Another method is to swing the boat directly into the wind. This safety valve method of releasing the sail is the quickest and most effective.

The method of determining if we are sailing as close into the wind as possible is to gradually turn the boat up into the direction of the wind until the outer edge of the sail begins to flutter. This indicates that we have sailed so directly into the wind that the wind is now blowing on both sides of the sail. When this occurs, the boat can be put back on course by simply pointing the nose of the boat away from the wind. Do not, under any circumstance, tie down the rope that is used to control the sail, nor is it advisable to loop the line around your hand. Should it become necessary to spill the wind, to avoid a capsize, it may be impossible for you to release the control line fast enough. Avoid sailing the boat too close into the wind since the forward motion will be considerably reduced.

SAILING DOWN WIND

After having arrived at our windward destination we now wish to go in the opposite direction, that is, with the wind on our back. A boat sailing in this manner can best be compared to a sled sliding downhill. The wind now "pushes" the boat in the downwind direction. In order to obtain maximum power from the wind, our sail is let out until it is approximately 90° to the center line of the boat. This is done to obtain full pressure of the wind against the greatest possible sail area. Extreme caution must be observed when sailing in this manner. If the person at the tiller is not alert and permits the boat to alter its course enough to allow the wind to blow behind the sail, there is the danger of the sail being flung from one side of the boat to the other. An action such as this is called a "jibe" and in this case an accidental jibe. The velocity reached by the boom during this swing is enough to cause a serious injury to anyone unfortunate enough to be caught in its path. The result of such an accident can do a great deal of damage to the boat such as a dismasting or can, in a rough sea, possibly capsize the boat. This can be avoided by a simple precaution.

Let us assume that we are sailing before the wind with the boom on the right-hand side of the boat. Rather than permit the wind to blow directly over to stern, veer the boat to the left so that the wind then blows over the left-hand shoulder of the man at the tiller. In this manner a safety zone is created which would permit a certain amount of wind shifting. Sailing with the wind striking the sail from over the shoulder of the helmsman is the best way to avoid an accidental jibe. By executing a series of controlled jibes it is possible to "tack downwind" in order to reach our downwind objective. We can best describe this maneuver by comparing it to the tacks we completed into the wind. In this case the wind is behind us rather than in front of us. Let us go through such a maneuver.

1. Our boat is sailing with the wind just over our left shoulder with the boom far out on the right side. We continue sailing on this tack until we find it necessary to change our direction in order to sail closer to our target, which is located to the right of our present course.

2. The next step is to haul in the mainsail, steadily and gradually, until the boom is directly over the center line of the boat.

3. Then swing the tiller away from the direction of the boom, drawing it toward the helmsman. The boat will then veer off to the right.

4. The man at the tiller swings the boat to the right until the wind is blowing directly from the back of the boat on both sides of the sail. At this point the boat is sailing on its momentum.

5. Continue to swing until the wind comes over your right shoulder.

6. At this point the sail is let out to assume the 90° angle on the left side of the boat.

In the beginning, this maneuver should be practiced only in the lightest breezes. It is difficult to execute this maneuver in a strong wind. The combination of steep waves and high winds make sailing before the wind a little tricky. Since you are traveling in the same direction as the wave, the boat behaves somewhat like a surf board.

There is a tendency on the part of the boat to swing broadside to the waves. When this happens, the boom which is extended out over the water, touches the wave, causing a tremendous drag on the rudder. This makes the boat unmaneuverable permitting the next wave that comes along to roll the boat over. By moving all ballast (passengers) as far back as possible the tendency of the boat to bury its nose and lift the rudder out of the water can be avoided.

In the beginning it is recommended that the centerboard remain down at all times to give the boat greater stability. Later, when you have achieved greater skill, the centerboard can be raised when running before the wind.

When it becomes necessary to return to a windward direction, it is a simple matter to swing the boat just as we do in tacking, by pushing the tiller to the boom. As the boat swings closer to the wind, haul the mainsail in gradually so that the boat does not lose forward motion. It is only necessary to continue the swing until the desired windward course is reached.

LANDING AT A MOORING

Basically, the principle involved in learning how to land at a mooring is that of being able to stop the forward motion of the boat.

The methods of landing at a dock or at a mooring are the same except that in the case of a mooring more speed can be tolerated since it is snagged with a boat hook and in this manner its forward motion can be checked.

1. Landing with the wind behind you: Assuming that you are approaching a long pier with a float at the end. Sail down wind until you are just about a boat length past the float; then tack up, heading the boat into the wind and utilizing the momentum to coast up to the float.

2. Landing with the wind coming from the dock: This requires that you sail on a reach (i. e., with the wind coming from your side) until the dock is about 45° from your course and about two boat lengths away. Then simply head up directly to the dock.

CAPSIZING

Distance is very deceptive on water and a shore line that seems apparently near could be miles away. The proper procedure in the event of a capsize is to:

1. Don your life preserver.

2. Get the anchor over to prevent drifting.

3. Remove sails from mast and boom.

4. By placing weight on centerboard and using it as a lever you can right boat.

5. Stuff the centerboard slot with a shirt or rag to prevent the boat from filling while you try to bail her out.

6. If this is not possible, hail a passing boat and you will be towed to shore and safety.

The willingness to help in time of distress is characteristic of seagoing folk.

By being aware of potential danger and observing the appropriate precautions, such danger will not readily materialize. •

Sail Slide Magazine

By S. S. Rabl

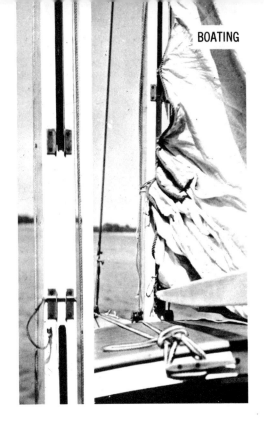

IF you've ever wished that you could slap a sail against the mast and hoist away without feeding the slides on the track one-by-one, here is a gimmick that will do the job for you.

The track on a new mast should be set away from the stick on a ¾x⅜ in. spruce liner along its entire length. On a mast already in use the lower end of the track should be linered out from nothing to ⅜-inch for about two feet. The drawing below shows the simple construction of one magazine. Where the sail is fastened also to the boom with slides, two magazines will be needed. •

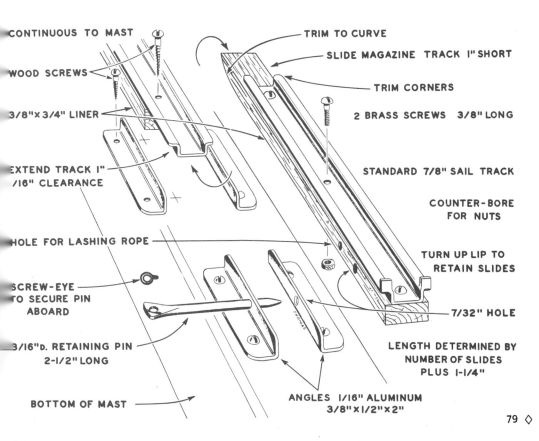

CONTINUOUS TO MAST

WOOD SCREWS

3/8"x 3/4" LINER

EXTEND TRACK 1"
/16" CLEARANCE

HOLE FOR LASHING ROPE

SCREW-EYE
TO SECURE PIN
ABOARD

3/16"D. RETAINING PIN
2-1/2" LONG

BOTTOM OF MAST

TRIM TO CURVE

SLIDE MAGAZINE TRACK 1" SHORT

TRIM CORNERS

2 BRASS SCREWS 3/8" LONG

STANDARD 7/8" SAIL TRACK

COUNTER-BORE
FOR NUTS

TURN UP LIP TO
RETAIN SLIDES

7/32" HOLE

LENGTH DETERMINED BY
NUMBER OF SLIDES
PLUS 1-1/4"

ANGLES 1/16" ALUMINUM
3/8"x1/2"x2"

Sail Care

Taking care of your sails properly will bring big rewards for very little effort.

By Ike Manchester

Properly broken in sails on Seagull above show perfect air-flow curve.

HOW many people realize that as much as one-fourth of the value of a small sailboat is invested in a good suit of sails? Probably not many, for despite a lot of good intentions, quite often sails are not given the simple but necessary care they must have in order to last out the life span built into them. Most owners of small boats willingly work hard to keep their crafts shipshape, but unfortunately, the same care is rarely given to a good set of sails.

To demonstrate a practical and effective routine of sail care, MECHANIX ILLUSTRATED asked the advice of Ike Manchester of the Manchester Yacht Sails Co., South Dartmouth, Mass., a well-known sailmaking concern. Mr. Manchester gives some simple rules for good sail care and shows how to carry them out.

New sail must be stretched gradually to make its specified length in order to acquire proper set.

Sails which are improperly broken in will never acquire a good set or operate really efficiently.

Feeding a sail into grooved mast is eased by furling the luff of the sail on top of the boom first.

Especially if sails are left on spars, use water and mildew-proof preservative for longer life.

Boom should come down amidships, preferably into boom crotch. Never lower your sails into water.

Always remove battens after a sail. They cause rips and tears in sails, can be broken if left in.

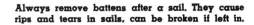

IF your boat hull is poorly maintained, it is quickly and obviously unseaworthy, and unsafe. But a neglected set of sails will still drive a boat after a fashion—not with much efficiency, though, and not for very long. A sparkling new paint job on your hull or a newly sanded deck will probably draw more attention than a well-maintained set of sails, but good sail care pays off in big dividends—maximum efficiency and substantially longer lasting performance for a very small cost in terms of time and money.

Any new sail should be stretched gradually to the length specified by the designer or sailmaker. If it is forced to its full length immediately, it will never acquire the set

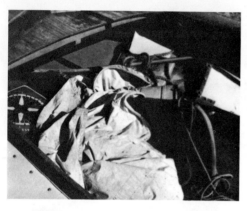

Nothing will cause sails to deteriorate more quickly than mildew. Sails left in boat bottom ask for it.

To prevent mildew as well as other sail damage, take sails off spars, carry ashore in sail bag.

Mildew fungus (above) needs dampness for growth, but does not affect synthetic fabrics like nylon.

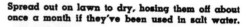

Spread out on lawn to dry, hosing them off about once a month if they've been used in salt water.

Dry sails indoors on rainy days. Hang them from line edges and in open position to keep shape.

When sail is dry, examine it carefully for rips, chafed spots, and loose fastenings (slides, etc.).

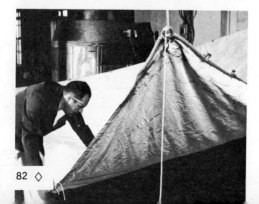

necessary for a perfect air-flow curve and top efficiency. Don't heave too heartily on the halyards the first few times out. Each sail should be stretched to size by the wind, not by the bully-boy action of a too-enthusiastic masthand. If you stretch your sail gradually in this way, it will automatically assume its proper set after a few sails.

When raising sails, careful feeding of the bolt rope or slides will help to prevent wrinkling and chafing of the sails.

Don't ever permit your sails to flap wildly if you can help it, for it causes severe wear and tear and can quickly do enough damage to require extensive sail repairs. You can avoid this unnecessary expense

Good sailors carry handy kits with waterproof tape, needle, and twine to make temporary repairs.

Check thoroughly at season's end to see if major repairs are needed. Have professional make them.

Folding sails properly, even thoroughly dry ones, is important to maintain shape. Make long folds . . .

... then roll neatly with as few creases as possible. Don't stretch the canvas. Leave lines exposed . . .

. . . like this, as oil and tar in them stains the sail. The neatly rolled sail is then tucked into sail bag.

Suspend bag from attic beam or in locker to keep rodents off. Wire is better than rope shown here.

by simply controlling your sails, especially in high winds.

Proper procedure in handling your sails after you've been for a sail is important. The boom should come down amidships, preferably into the boom crotch.

Remove your sails from the spars and take out the battens. Left in, they can cause rips and tears as well as be broken themselves. Sails should then be taken ashore and spread on the lawn or hung indoors to dry thoroughly.

Sails should be examined frequently for small rips and tears which, if mended immediately, will save more extensive repairwork later. This is another very good example of the proverbial ounce of prevention being worth many dollars of cure, for little rips can be whipped into giant tears by just one sail on a blustery day. A sail-mending kit which contains needle, twine, and waterproof tape is a very convenient item to keep around. At the end of each season, you should examine all your sails carefully.

Sails should be dried, folded, and stored as shown in the photographs. Leaving them in heaps at the bottom of your boat, folding them before they have thoroughly dried, or letting them remain on the rigging during rain, morning fogs, etc., is just asking for them to mildew. This fungus growth which thrives on dampness is most detrimental to any canvas, silk, or cotton sail, for it causes very rapid deterioration. Mildew does not affect the synthetic fabrics like nylon, but poor treatment of even such hardy fabrics will wear them out much more quickly than is necessary.

If you use your sailboat so frequently that you want to leave the sails rigged, you should give them a good coat of one of the water and mildew-proof preservatives which ought to be brushed on sails at the beginning of the season for best protection.

Lastly, store your repaired and carefully folded sails in your sailbag which should be suspended from a wire (it precludes any possibility of rats or mice getting at them) and hung in a dry place. •

boating hints

Practical Scupper Strainers. The commonly used flat strainer with holes in the top clogs up with trash and small particles very quickly. This results in a large pool of water on deck and more in the bilge. To eliminate this annoyance, I designed and built a brass cone, hammered a flange around the edge, soldered a ⅛-in.-dia. brass rod across the top for a handle, and drilled the cone full of ⅛-in. holes. The bottom of the cone forms a basin where trash can collect without stopping the flow of water. The strainer is easily lifted out for cleaning. The pattern is for a cone that will fit a 1½-in. scupper.—*George Brook Taylor.*

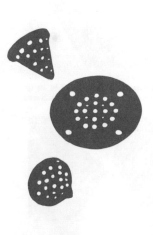

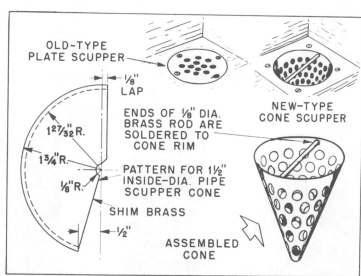

OLD-TYPE PLATE SCUPPER

⅛" LAP

1 27/32" R.

1 ¾" R.

⅛" R.

½"

ENDS OF ⅛" DIA. BRASS ROD ARE SOLDERED TO CONE RIM

PATTERN FOR 1½" INSIDE-DIA. PIPE SCUPPER CONE

SHIM BRASS

NEW-TYPE CONE SCUPPER

ASSEMBLED CONE

Inertia-Operated Pump

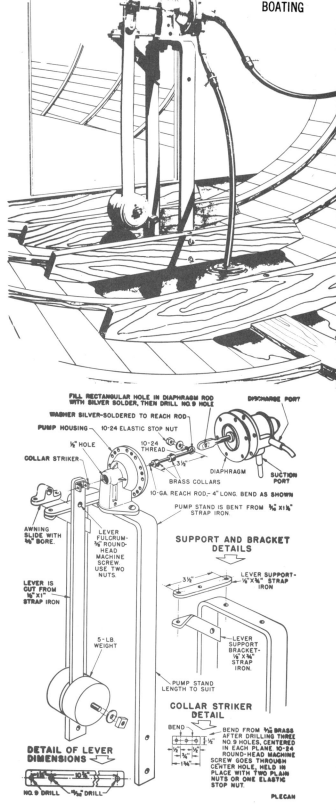

WEEK-END sailors will enjoy peace of mind if they know the water from normal seepage during the week is squirting overboard with every roll of their boats. With an average of six strokes per minute, this pump will move 30 gallons a day.

Purchase a secondhand fuel pump without a vacuum-booster chamber. Disassemble and thoroughly clean it and add new valves, valve springs, diaphragm, and gaskets. Omit the diaphragm return spring. Solder up the rectangular hole in the diaphragm rod; then drill a No. 9 hole for the reach rod. Drill a ½-in. hole in the pump housing for insertion of the reach rod. The reach rod and collars are taken from Junior's Erector set. Bend the rod as shown and silver-solder a small washer at the bend. Thread the short end of the rod for a nut. Replace the pump screen with one cut from bronze window screening, which will provide sufficient protection for bilge service. Assemble and check the pump.

The lever is 12¾ in. long; drill it as shown. Make the collar striker and fasten it to the top of the lever so it is free to rotate. The counterweight can be cast from lead or built up from 3-in. plate washers. Make the pump stand to suit and bolt it to two adjacent frames so the lever swings athwartships. Bolt the pump in place and add the lever support, the lever-support bracket, the awning-slide lever bearing, and the lever. Set the reach-rod collars ⅛ in. from the ends of the striker.

Pipe up the pump with $\frac{5}{16}$-in. rubber hose over $\frac{5}{16}$-in. copper tubing fitted to the pump ports. Use bronze screening to form a bonnet over the end of the suction line.
—R. Lieto ●

FILL RECTANGULAR HOLE IN DIAPHRAGM ROD WITH SILVER SOLDER, THEN DRILL NO. 9 HOLE

DISCHARGE PORT

WASHER SILVER-SOLDERED TO REACH ROD

PUMP HOUSING — 10-24 ELASTIC STOP NUT

½" HOLE

COLLAR STRIKER

10-24 THREAD

3½"

DIAPHRAGM

SUCTION PORT

BRASS COLLARS

10-GA. REACH ROD,— 4" LONG. BEND AS SHOWN

PUMP STAND IS BENT FROM ⁵⁄₁₆" X ⅛" STRAP IRON.

AWNING SLIDE WITH ¼" BORE.

LEVER FULCRUM— ⅜" ROUND-HEAD MACHINE SCREW. USE TWO NUTS.

LEVER IS CUT FROM ⅛" X 1" STRAP IRON

5-LB. WEIGHT

SUPPORT AND BRACKET DETAILS

3½"

LEVER SUPPORT- ⅛" X ¾" STRAP IRON

LEVER SUPPORT BRACKET- ⅛" X ¾" STRAP IRON.

PUMP STAND LENGTH TO SUIT

COLLAR STRIKER DETAIL

BEND

1½"

½"   1½"

¾"

1¾"

BEND FROM ⁵⁄₁₆" BRASS AFTER DRILLING THREE NO. 9 HOLES, CENTERED IN EACH PLANE. 10-24 ROUND-HEAD MACHINE SCREW GOES THROUGH CENTER HOLE, HELD IN PLACE WITH TWO PLAIN NUTS OR ONE ELASTIC STOP NUT.

DETAIL OF LEVER DIMENSIONS

10¼"

NO. 9 DRILL   ⁵⁄₃₂" DRILL

PLECAN

Rigging a Small Sailboat

Make a boat safer and easier to handle by leading all lines close to the tiller.

By John Wolbarst

IT often happens that small sailboats aren't rigged for maximum safety and ease of handling. The jib and mainsail halyards, for instance, are usually cleated to the base of the mast. This means that it's necessary to get up, leave the tiller and go forward if you want to drop sail in a hurry. Then too, dual jib sheets, used with an overlapping jib, often lead back to cleats along the rails. In a stiff wind, with the crew up to windward to keep the boat down, the jib sheet in use is cleated out of reach across the cockpit. Trouble may arise in a sudden squall or if the boat grounds and the helmsman can't act quickly and smoothly. After a near accident in my 14-ft. plywood centerboarder, I re-rigged the boat as follows:

Halyards: Two small cheek blocks were added, one each side, near the base of the mast. The jib and mainsail halyards run through these and aft to the cleats.

Mainsheet: This formerly came down from the boom to the rear of the centerboard box, was in the way when coming about and led off in different directions, depending upon which tack the boat was on. A pulley on the boom was moved forward two feet and a swivel pulley mounted on the centerboard box directly beneath it. The sheet now goes forward along the boom, down to the pulley on the box and aft to a jam cleat.

Jib sheets: The dual sheets now pass through swivel pulleys on the rails and lead to a cleat at the center.

Jib downhaul: A light line was run from the head of the jib, along the jib-

All lines lead back to a central location atop thwart mounted at the rear of the centerboard box. It's easy for lone sailor to drop sails quickly when necessary.

Downhaul is run down jibstay inside snaps and then passes through a shackle at the bow.

stay inside all jib snaps, through the shackle at the bow and aft to a cleat. This was done because the jib is too light to fall by itself. Now I turn the boat into the wind briefly, center the sail over the boat, let go the jib halyard and give a few pulls on the downhaul. The jib comes into the boat and I never leave the tiller.

Now, having everything at hand when an emergency comes up, both sails can be dropped within 45 seconds. The cost of this added safety and convenience was only a few dollars. •

Manner in which the boat was rerigged is detailed below. Jib sheet in use is cleated.

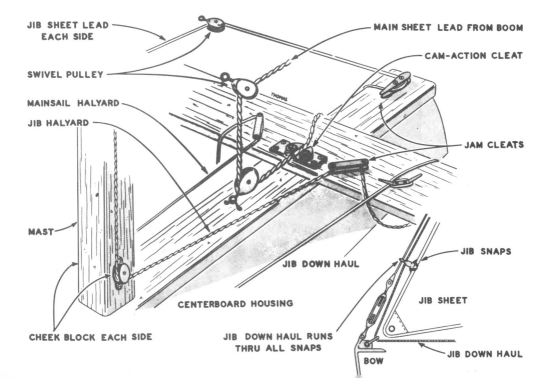

JIB SHEET LEAD EACH SIDE

MAIN SHEET LEAD FROM BOOM

CAM-ACTION CLEAT

SWIVEL PULLEY

THOMAS

MAINSAIL HALYARD

JIB HALYARD

JAM CLEATS

MAST

JIB SNAPS

JIB DOWN HAUL

JIB SHEET

CENTERBOARD HOUSING

CHEEK BLOCK EACH SIDE

JIB DOWN HAUL RUNS THRU ALL SNAPS

JIB DOWN HAUL

BOW

Outboard Motor Cart

Those big, heavy outboards are easy to handle with a cart like this.

By Howard Rozelle

THIS outboard motor cart has everything. It's strong enough to handle a 40-horsepower engine; it's rigid enough to allow it to be used as a repair stand, even to cranking; it hauls a gas tank, with room left for a tool box; it's so well balanced that a child or a woman can move a big engine easily; and it folds compactly in 10 seconds by removing one pin which also locks it in the folded position. What's more it's light, easy to build and cheap.

If the materials are salvaged from scrapped toys and discarded pieces of pipe, it can be built for as little as $3.75.

Even if used materials are purchased and spot welding is paid for, the cost shouldn't exceed seven dollars. A cart incorporating all its features would sell for a good deal more.

The simple construction is detailed in the drawing. Beyond what is shown, little information is required. Note, in the illustration at the upper right of the next page, that the handles are bent outward. The width at the pivot is only 19½ in.—slightly too narrow. A few inches above the pivot, the pipes are bent so that the width at the ends of the handles is 22 in. Another thing that bears mention is that the hole in the outer pipe at the pivot should be reamed slightly larger to allow for the bolt wobble caused by the bend of the pipes at this point.

Wheels are 10-in. diameter, but 8 or 12-in. may be used if slight alterations are made in the dimensions. The axles are mounted in holes drilled through the support pipes and then spot welded. Hub caps are used as dressing.

Pipes must be threaded where elbows are used at the joints. Spot welding is used elsewhere. The crosspiece beneath the wooden mount is cut to size and welded in position where the U brackets will engage it when the cart is folded.

Vertical tabs, welded at the ends of the platform, prevent a gas tank or tool box from sliding off. •

Cart is tilted up to show how single cotter pin (through U bracket) locks platform to bottom rear crosspiece.

Remove cotter pin, lift platform and swing sections together to fold cart. Pin is replaced at center crosspiece.

BILL OF MATERIALS

Used Pipe: ¾" dia., 20'
Electrical Conduit: ½" dia., 9'
Bolts: 4, ½"x2"
      2, ⅜"x3"
Strap Iron: ⅛"x1", 5" long
Pipe Elbows: 4, ¾" I.D.
Axles: 2 long bolts (or a steel rod) at least ½" dia.
Plywood: 1 piece, ¾"x5"x18"
        1 piece, ¾"x5"x16½"
Wheels, 10" dia.; hub caps; grips

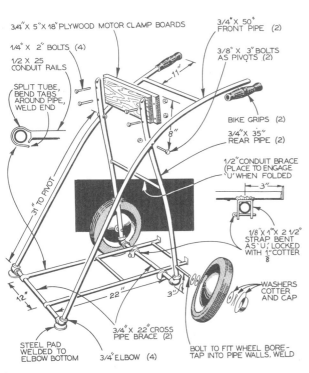

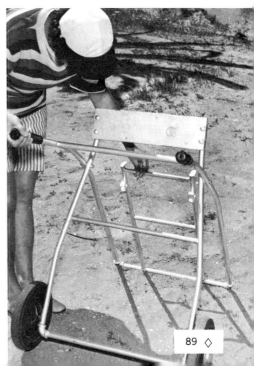

Boat Windshield

For the boatman who has been looking for an inexpensive windshield, here is one that should answer all his needs.

By Joseph Adams

A windshield on an outboard runabout has two purposes; it keeps out spray and is a must if a top is to be installed in the boat.

The dimensions shown on the drawing are for a broad 16-footer and they should be adjusted according to the length and width of your particular boat. The glass is V-type, shatterproof auto glass, obtainable from auto wreckers for about $5 a section. Score the glass on both sides, and with one edge raised slightly, tap along the score with a hammer. The inner gummy layer is then cut with a razor blade.

The frame should be made from the same type wood as the deck and stained to match the general appearance of your boat. Waterproof glue is used throughout. To avoid moisture between glass and framework use elastic seam composition. To make a good contact between deck and windshield, a piece of electrician's tape should be cemented to the underside of the windshield frame.

Marine grade plywood and brass screws should be used for best durability. The finished windshield will cost about $10 as compared to the $50 paid for most commercial ones. •

A band saw or portable jig saw will easily cut the plywood frame to the desired shape.

Front and center sections are permanently joined. The back section is removable.

To get the proper contour, set frame up as shown and trace deck shape with a compass.

After frame is sanded to conform to deck, the side braces are attached with brass screws.

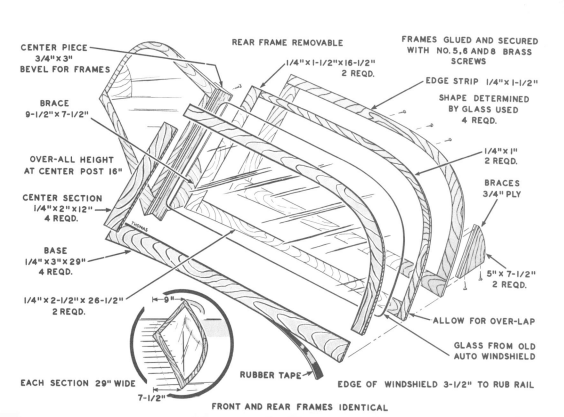

CENTER PIECE
3/4" x 3"
BEVEL FOR FRAMES

REAR FRAME REMOVABLE

1/4" x 1-1/2" x 16-1/2"
2 REQD.

FRAMES GLUED AND SECURED
WITH NO. 5, 6 AND 8 BRASS
SCREWS

EDGE STRIP 1/4" x 1-1/2"
SHAPE DETERMINED
BY GLASS USED
4 REQD.

BRACE
9-1/2" x 7-1/2"

OVER-ALL HEIGHT
AT CENTER POST 16"

CENTER SECTION
1/4" x 2" x 12"
4 REQD.

THOMAS

1/4" x 1"
2 REQD.

BRACES
3/4" PLY

BASE
1/4" x 3" x 29"
4 REQD.

5" x 7-1/2"
2 REQD.

1/4" x 2-1/2" x 26-1/2"
2 REQD.

9"

ALLOW FOR OVER-LAP

GLASS FROM OLD
AUTO WINDSHIELD

EACH SECTION 29" WIDE

7-1/2"

RUBBER TAPE

EDGE OF WINDSHIELD 3-1/2" TO RUB RAIL

FRONT AND REAR FRAMES IDENTICAL

Detachable Outboard Cabin

Now you can convert your open runabout into an outboard cruiser using this inexpensive design.

THIS lightweight cabin will provide you with a dual-purpose boat, an open craft for calm inland water, or weather-and-spray protection where the going is rough. It can be lifted off by removing seven bolts. The original was built on a farm with a circular saw the only power equipment available.

Front view of the easily built cabin shows framed plate glass windshield.

By Hi Sibley

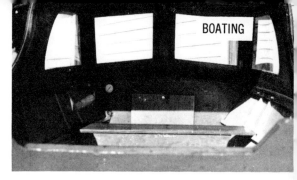

Three-quarter view shows amazing roominess of the portable cabin. Note plywood forward deck.

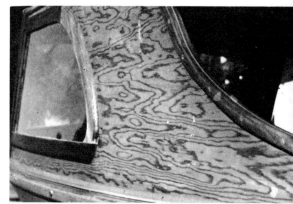

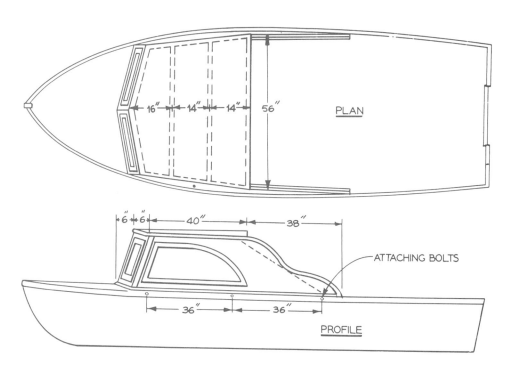

16"   14"   14"   56"   PLAN

6" 6"   40"   38"

ATTACHING BOLTS

36"   36"

PROFILE

General over-all dimensions are given in the plan and profile drawings as adapted to a standard 15-ft. Fiberglas hull. Dimensions can and should be adjusted to fit your own boat. Assembly details are shown also in the drawings.

Sides are ½-in. marine plywood reinforced with ¾-in. mahogany framing with 1⅛-in. carlins supporting the cabin roof. This is the same material as the sides and is secured with seven ovalhead screws in each beam. Apply waterproof glue to all contacting surfaces.

Application of retaining bolt also is illustrated. Brass toilet bolts are used in the original, with nuts on the inside. The only preparations necessary on the hull are to drill holes for the bolts through rub rail and sheer stringer, and deck over the bow end with a 2x2-in. stringer underneath, running fore-and-aft, to which the seventh bolt is secured, as shown in the drawing. This view also gives locations of bolts with nuts on the inside and heads countersunk and plugged over with shipwright's dowels. Note bulkhead which is secured to ribs, either existing in this location or added. Ample storage space is thus provided and, with a Fiberglas hull, will be dry. This type of hull just doesn't leak. In case your hull is open forward, deck it over with ¼-in. marine plywood, installing beams similar to the carlins of the roof. Seal the joint at the sheer line with marine glue.

The windshield sash consists of mahogany framing with ¼-in. plate glass and are hung at the top with brass piano hinges. Catches are provided on the inside with folding brackets to hold them open when ventilation is desired.

Profile on the side wall is given in the last drawing. One-inch half-round molding is installed along the top edge with cove molding along the bottom. Window frame is rabbeted for the plate glass, straight sections being cut with the power saw, curved parts chiseled out. •

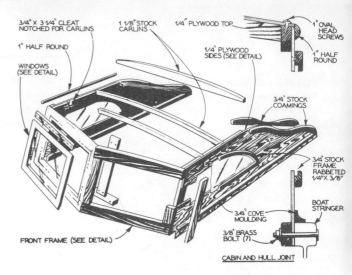

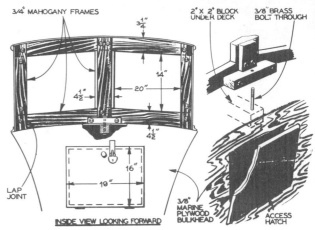

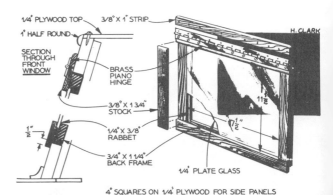

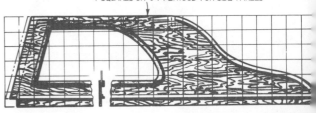

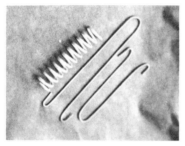

You can keep your canvas boat cover snug with this simple gadget made out of a strong compression spring and two pieces of wire or bronze welding rod as shown in photo left.

A rope buffer on your dinghy will protect the paint of your sloop or cruiser. Rope should be stretched prior to attaching it.

Ordinary garden hose, 12 to 18 inches long, and split spiral fashion can be slipped over mooring line to make a good chafing gear.

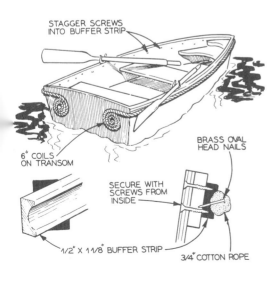

STAGGER SCREWS INTO BUFFER STRIP

6" COILS ON TRANSOM

SECURE WITH SCREWS FROM INSIDE

BRASS OVAL HEAD NAILS

1/2" X 11/8" BUFFER STRIP

3/4" COTTON ROPE

SLIT SPIRALLY TO RETAIN HOLD ON ROPE

Enclosing the Outboard

Keep out a following sea and tone down the noise
by enclosing the outboard in a self-bailing well.

By F. C. Clark

THE transom cut for the engine on many an outboard cruiser is so low that a following sea has no trouble climbing into the boat. No matter how good the skipper's intentions, there are times when he's caught out in rough weather and the low cut becomes dangerous.

I've found that the best answer is to merely enclose the engine on three sides with lockers and a self-bailing well. At first thought, an enclosure running the full width of the cockpit, and extending some 20 in. inboard of the transom, may seem to take up too much space in an area already small. In practice, however, such an arrangement actually added to the size of the boat by providing for the orderly housing of cables and gear. In addition, appearance was improved and motor noise deadened. Fiberglas or Stryofoam insulation in the well will deaden the noise even more.

Dimensions of the enclosure will vary, depending on the boat and motor. Just mount the motor (or motors) on the transom and run through all tilts and swings—size of the enclosure will be obvious. Remember drain holes at rear of well and ventilate properly, else the engine will cough and die. •

A
20"
17*
HINGED FOR MOTOR ACCESS
15½"
16"

* IF THIS DIMENSION IS NOT 17"OR MORE, ADD CURVED HOOD OR BRIDGE DECK 'A'

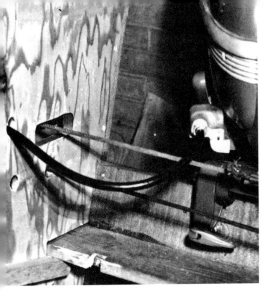

Gas line and steering cable holes. Shape opening so that steering cable won't rub.

Top panel of false transom is folded down, outboard clamped inboard for trailer move.

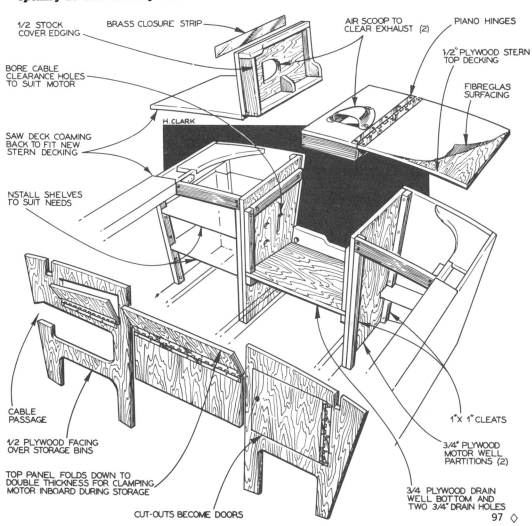

1/2 STOCK COVER EDGING

BRASS CLOSURE STRIP

AIR SCOOP TO CLEAR EXHAUST (2)

PIANO HINGES

1/2" PLYWOOD STERN TOP DECKING

BORE CABLE CLEARANCE HOLES TO SUIT MOTOR

FIBREGLAS SURFACING

H. CLARK

SAW DECK COAMING BACK TO FIT NEW STERN DECKING

NSTALL SHELVES TO SUIT NEEDS

CABLE PASSAGE

1/2 PLYWOOD FACING OVER STORAGE BINS

TOP PANEL FOLDS DOWN TO DOUBLE THICKNESS FOR CLAMPING MOTOR INBOARD DURING STORAGE

CUT-OUTS BECOME DOORS

1"X 1" CLEATS

3/4" PLYWOOD MOTOR WELL PARTITIONS (2)

3/4 PLYWOOD DRAIN WELL BOTTOM AND TWO 3/4" DRAIN HOLES

Photos by the author

Above a plywood runabout is shown in action. Usually driver takes more punishment than boat.

Hull Repair

Here is a simple procedure for replacing a plywood planked bottom. The only power-driven tool you need on the job is an electric drill.

As can be seen in a stern view of badly damaged bottom, the aluminum fin was completely torn off.

Wood dough over screw head must first be removed with ice pick or other sharp instrument.

DURING the past ten years, plywood planking has been used on more and more boats. Better waterproof glue and improved manufacturing methods have turned plywood into a very durable material. The small runabout pictured, which is capable of doing over 50 miles per hour, has only ¼-in. thick plywood on the bottom and weighs less than 140 pounds. This little boat flipped the driver and ran up on a rocky shore line. Although not punctured, the bottom was ruined.

The repair time on the project was 15 hours—from removing the old bottom to replacing the new one and finishing it off. Cost was $16.00 for 4x10-ft. mahogany plywood and $12.00 for paint and screws. The bottom on this particular boat was glued and screwed to all the battens and chines, and in some places Anchorfast nails were used. Most small boats are built the same way except that Bedlast or some other sealer may be used in place of glue. In any case the procedure for repairing remains the same.

Place the boat, bottom up, on a pair of padded saw horses of a good workable height. Then remove all screws and nails. Dig out the wood dough over the screw heads with a sharp instrument such as an ice pick and unscrew them. Anchorfast nails are best handled by cutting the wood from around them with a sharp chisel and using a claw hammer to pull them out. If the screws are brass, the chances are that you can use them again, but the nails are a total loss.

With the boat right side up on the horses, pound the bottom out with a blunt block of wood and a husky hammer. Be sure that the part of the bottom you are working on is not directly over the horses. After the bottom has been loosened from the frame, turn upside down and remove the entire bottom. With a little care it will remain in one piece, and can be used as a pattern for the new bottom.

Turn the boat upside down again and clean off all the battens and stringers which the bottom will contact. If the bottom was glued you will have one layer of the plywood adhering to the frame. This is best removed with a hand plane. The plane blade will easily cut off the remaining plywood without going through the glue. Using a straightedge, check the frame to see that it is flat and true.

Using the old bottom as a template, cut out your new bottom to size leaving a little extra to be trimmed off after it is attached in place. I used ¼-in. thick mahogany instead of the old ¼-in. fir plywood. The mahogany costs more but stands up better and does not require the sizing fir plywood needs. I used Sealer 900 between the plywood and frame. The bottom is carefully fitted in place and notched up front where it comes to a vee. All the pilot holes for the screws or Anchorfast nails are drilled now.

Remove the bottom and dust off the sawdust from the pilot holes, and generously coat the battens and chines with Weldwood glue or a good sealer—whatever you prefer. The bottom is now quickly screwed or nailed in place, about every two inches on the chines and transom and 4 inches apart on all battens. If screws are used, a

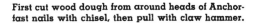

After the slit in the screw is completely clean, it's easy enough to remove screw with screwdriver.

First cut wood dough from around heads of Anchorfast nails with chisel, then pull with claw hammer.

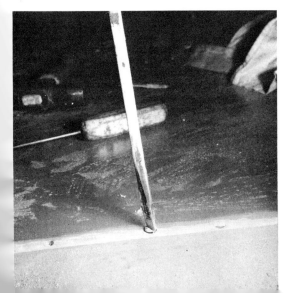

Pound out the bottom with block of wood and hammer. Make sure saw horse is not directly beneath.

After loosening bottom from frame, turn boat upside down and remove bottom, keeping it intact.

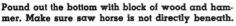

Plane off pieces of plywood which are stuck to frame. Use your steel straightedge as check on level.

Screw holes are drilled with a "screwmate" which drills tapered holes and countersinks for heads.

Oscillating sander is handy for smoothing bottom and wet sanding it, after the last coat of paint.

screw attachment for a small electric drill will save time and blisters on your hands. Wood dough is used over all the countersunk screwheads, or nails.

When the wood dough and glue is dry, trim off the excess and sand down the entire bottom with a medium fine paper. If the bottom is fir plywood your best bet is to use a sealer like white Firzite before painting. Use a good boat enamel. I used Boat Life, and after two coats I wet sanded to a slick finish. If the boat is to be used in fresh water only a good outdoor enamel will do the trick.

If mahogany is used no sealer is needed. Don't forget to give the inside of the bottom a coat of varnish or paint. Your Runabout is now as good as new and ready for action. ●

Bill of Materials

4x10 ft. sheet of ¼ in. marine plywood (mahogany or fir)
3 gross of ⅞ No. 7 screws or 1 pound of 1 in. No. 12 Anchorfast nails (350 nails per pound)
1 pound of Weldwood glue or one quart of Sealer 900
1 quart Spar varnish for inside of boat
1 quart Boat Life or Spar varnish for outside
1 quart of Firzite if fir plywood is used
Small can of wood dough

Here finished bottom gets its final coat of paint. Inside of bottom will take either paint or varnish.

PEANUT

BEVELING entire frame for application of plywood skin. Stanley Surform file does precision job easily. Note fairing stick, above, used for checking out the bevels.

YOU CAN KILL TWO BIRDS with this project: Learn how to go about this business of making a boat from plans—and also to provide your little guy with one of the proudest life-size "toys" a kid ever had. You can build this little nifty in a couple of weekends and for less than twenty bucks. My boy is only eight and he loves it. With a helmet on he's a king at the controls, the envy of every kid in the county—and the darling of the ladies. I nearly busted my bib with pride when I first saw him take off in it.

With the "Fisherman's Friend," the 3 hp Evinrude kicker which usually trolls, this baby takes off like a hydro. Does a smart 15 mph or better.

Built of ⅛-inch plywood, the boat weighs about 35 lbs. With the motor off it

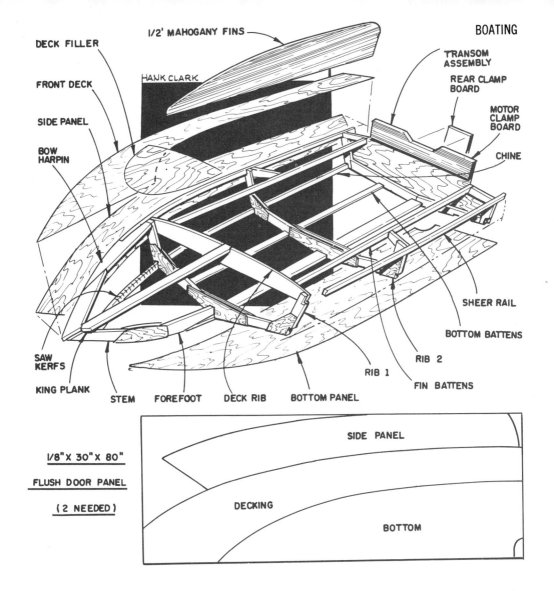

1/2' MAHOGANY FINS

DECK FILLER

FRONT DECK

SIDE PANEL

BOW HARPIN

HANK CLARK

TRANSOM ASSEMBLY

REAR CLAMP BOARD

MOTOR CLAMP BOARD

CHINE

SHEER RAIL

BOTTOM BATTENS

RIB 2

RIB 1

FIN BATTENS

SAW KERFS

KING PLANK

STEM

FOREFOOT

DECK RIB

BOTTOM PANEL

1/8"X 30"X 80"

FLUSH DOOR PANEL

(2 NEEDED)

SIDE PANEL

DECKING

BOTTOM

can carry an adult, the action gained by holding onto a tow rope a la water skiing. Lots of fun here. Foreward driving is obtained by re-rigging the fuel feed, substituting a car choke cable to create a remote fuel feed.

Assemble the two little ribs first (about an hour's work) and you will find there's still time to make the transom in one evening. Lay out all the cut stock over the full-size rib plans, then put together with gussets, glue and nails. Transom is 1/8-inch ply plank, edged with 3/8-inch fir. Nail through the ply into the fir, using glue. Now cut the stem and forefoot stock, with band or jig saw, to curve, and join with ply gusset. Bow harpin is next, and is used because the sheer rail could never bend so sharply. Jig saw solid fir into curve, and

join halves with plywood web under. Now for the jig setup. This is two rails of 2x4 onto which are placed all ribs, transom, stem, and harpin. Nail a 1x2 across both ribs for support upside down on the rails. Space ribs, using keelson piece with clamps. Screw stem top to harpin, nail harpin to jig, join with keelson, which goes back to transom notch. Transom tilts 5 inches forward. After checking line up, drive a screw into each rib through the keelson, using glue liberally. Now add the sheer rails, screwing first to harpin's edge. Then bend back to transom notch with one screw per rib.

Now comes a more difficult area of work, bending on the chines, over which the side and bottom panels join. From transom to Rib 1, o.k. but from there to stem the bend is too much for the ¾-inch mahogany. You could use fir, but this doesn't hold nails like mahogany. Solution is to cut a series of saw kerfs along the inside face of the chine, relieving the compressed grain. Then it bends readily. Water won't help. Space the cuts about ½ inch apart. As you bend toward the stem, plane on the bevel where the bottom ·ply lays, then secure with screws and glue to all ribs and stem. Now bevel all the chine, stem, and transom for good contacts of bottom and side ply panels, using a flexible stick to check your planing. Keelson also gets beveled in the process. Actually, you must fuss with this job as you would on any larger boat hull, since this is meant to keep water out with tight joints.

Now cut and place the two bottom battens into their notches, and secure using glue and screws. For planking, we used ⅛-inch mahogany plywood from flush door stock, getting all parts out of two sheets, 30x80 inches. Use a 4 by 8-ft. panel if that's available, and get all parts except deck out of one sheet. If ⅛ is not available, use ¼-inch plywood, but this will make the boat heavier and overly strong, and require much wetting around the stem bend. But it can be used. The side panels go on first as usual and are blanked out by following the figures given on the large scale art. Clamp a side panel to the frame,

check for fit and lay, then put in about four pilot screws, as a position gauge. Then remove, swab with Weldwood glue along chine, sheers, and stem, then replace panel with the pilot screws. Immediately start driving in the aluminum nails every two inches along chine, stem and transom, and 3 inches along sheer. Anchorfast nails are fine, too, but the glues does the real holding job. Repeat this process for the other side, and for the two bottom panels. Bottom panels extend about 5 inches aft of transom bottom as afterplane. Use a back-up block when nailing into the chine forward of Rib 1, as the kerfs make it somewhat flexible until the glue all sets. Later when turning the boat over, work filler into these kerfs with a putty knife, a good Weldwood and saw dust mix, with water. Knock off the jig now, along with rib ties, and set the hull upright.

After taking pictures of Junior in it, remove the boy, and beg him to let you install the deck dash, followed by the fin battens back to the transom. Install the motor clamp now using plenty of glue, and back this up with the rear clamp board. Avoid nails here, and use clamps. Cut the decks out of the ⅛-inch plywood remaining and lay on with glue and nails. Trim, when dry, along the gunwales, and along fin batten. Plane the fin batten to a vertical plane, so that fin stands erect or vertical

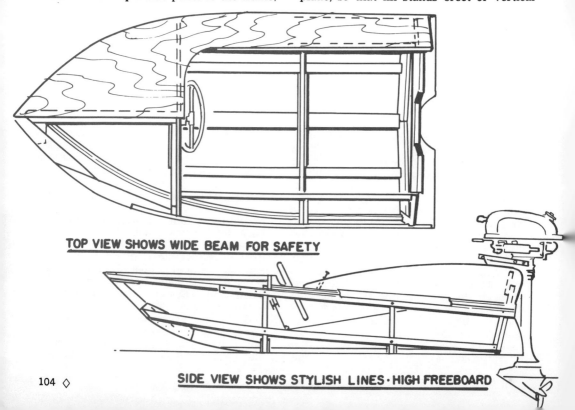

TOP VIEW SHOWS WIDE BEAM FOR SAFETY

SIDE VIEW SHOWS STYLISH LINES · HIGH FREEBOARD

when glued and screwed in next. This fin also braces the transom motor board. Two long screws driven through it into the board, along with generous glue, do the job. Thus you have adequate freeboard for safety, and the new finny look. Screws go every 8 inches along fin into batten. Now place glue blocks along the seams behind the transom, at bottom and sides to assist in waterproofing. Now you can varnish the hull if mahogany, or paint to taste.

Clamp on the 3 hp Evinrude, hook up the choke control, the steering, a quick removal device on drawings, and Junior can take off just like dad does. Watch the gas, because one pull sends the engine into drive, as there is no gear shift. Just aim away from everything, and in idle, the boat maneuvers slowly and surely.

One caution: Do not lean back against the motor at idle, since the boat will be end heavy then. Balance with the bricks. Under all circumstances, an elder should be watching. The boat is capable. Be sure the boy is. It's tremendous fun when all hands know what's what. •

SPECIFICATIONS

Length ....6 ft.
Beam ....35 in.
Depth ....12 in.
Freeboard ....9 in.
Weight ....35 lbs.

BILL OF MATERIALS

FIR

¾"x2"x12'	Ribs-Transom
1⅛"x2"x36"	Stem-Forefoot
¾"x3"x88"	Harpin
¾"x1"x80"	Fin Battens
¾"x3"x32"	Dash
Weldwood Resin Powder	

MAHOGANY

¾"x4"x22"	Motor Clamp
¾"x6"x12"	Rear Clamp
½"x1"x16'	Sheers-Battens
⅝"x1"x12'	Chines
¾"x2"x48"	Keelson
½"x8"x5'	Fins

PLYWOOD (Mahogany)

⅛"x30"x80"	(From Flush Door)
(or 4'x8' panel)	
⅛"x12"x33"	Transom
⅛"x12"x20"	Gussets
¼"x6"x32"	Bottom Gussets

HARDWARE

1½" No. 7	3 Doz.
1" No. 6	1 Doz.
1 Lb. ½"	Brads
5 Lb. ⅝"	Aluminum Nails (Planking)

LARGE SCALE PLANS

with full size half ribs are available for building this boat at $3.00 per set. Send orders to Henry Clark, 36 Highwood Drive, Dumont, N. J. 07628. Specify FB-PEANUT.

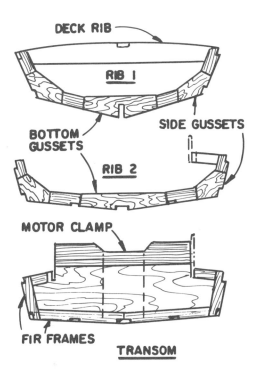

DECK RIB

RIB I

BOTTOM GUSSETS

SIDE GUSSETS

RIB 2

MOTOR CLAMP

FIR FRAMES

TRANSOM

ROWBOAT

Make it for $50 from one piece of plywood

THIS 11-foot hull will cost you only $50 to build and comes out of a single sheet of ⅜-inch plywood. We used Weldwood Royal Marine Plywood for the job. It can be put together by almost any workshopper with a minimum amount of tools and time.

It rows smartly and gets a real burst of speed from a 3 to 5-hp outboard, actually planing like a runabout. It won't tip or trip with its generously flared sides and will take a rough clop. It can be lifted on top of a car by one man. It will carry up to four persons. The editors feel that it's im-possible to get so much water transport anywhere for so little cost.

In cutting and assembly, you deal directly with the planking, first and last. Except for the transom, no other ribs are used. No precision jigging, alignments, plumbs, squares, angles, rakes, deadrise, coordinates, lofting or full-size layout is necessary. It can be done in a weekend, or if you prefer to work leisurely, two weekends.

In addition to the materials mentioned, tools required or helpful are as follows:

Glue bottom batten for assembly to the transom bottom. The top batten goes on the same way, is screwed from the back.

Photo at left shows the transom as seen on a jig, with the two side panels screwed lightly to it for bend trials; cord tacks front end, as shown here.

a rip saw or saber, plane, ratchet screwdriver, Stanley's Surform (extremely handy for planing jobs), an electric drill with Screwmate.

The author tested the boat on Long Island Sound, using a 3-hp Evinrude Lightwin and a 5-hp Evinrude Fisherman. With the 5 attached, the boat climbed right out on a plane and clocked 17 mph with two persons aboard! With the Fisherman at full bore, the bow was rammed through every large wake available; it either parted through or planed right across the ridge of

each. As a small scale runabout, this is a superb boat; it handles easily and offers real boating thrills, yet isn't overly much for even a child to handle. It makes a dandy second boat for every member of the family to enjoy.

When finishing, seal all plywood with Firzite or other filler and varnish or enamel to suit. Before beginning, study the drawings carefully, then study the step-by-step photographs. It's a simple boat to construct. And it'll offer a summer full of fun. Why not begin now? •

BILL OF MATERIALS

3/8"x4'x14' marine plywood
(one)
1"x3"x13" mahogany (keel and
lower transom batten)
1"x1½"x10' mahogany (2)
(chines)
1"x1¼"x11' mahogany (2)
(shear)
1"x1¼"x10' mahogany (1) (keel)
2"x2"x12" inner stem (1)
1"x6"x60" transom top and
knees
1"x10"x48" seat (1)
1"x12"x48" seat (1)
1 lb. Weldwood waterproof glue
3/4" no. 7 Screw-mate
2 gross 7/8" no. 7 brass screws
40 1¼" no. 8 brass screws

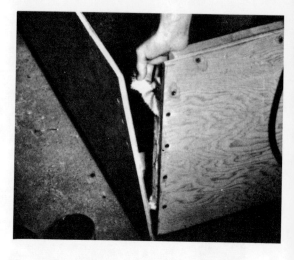

After drilling the sides for screws, glue them
to the transom batten. Into the glue bed, lay
linen strip which compresses, distributing the
Weldwood marine glue entirely over the surfaces.

(NUMBERS ARE IN ORDER OF ASSEMBLY)

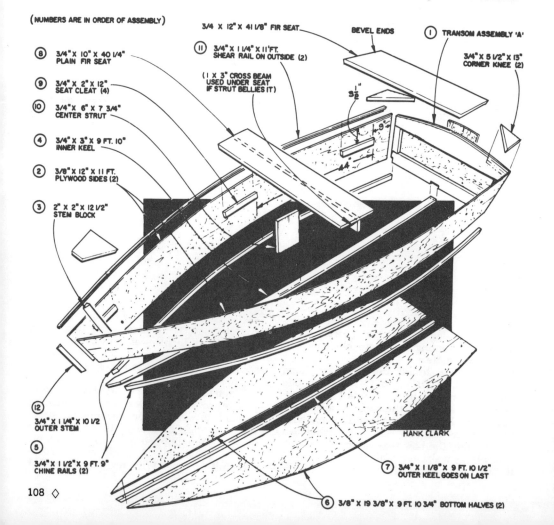

3/4 X 12" X 41 1/8" FIR SEAT

BEVEL ENDS

① TRANSOM ASSEMBLY 'A'

⑧ 3/4" X 10" X 40 1/4"
PLAIN FIR SEAT

⑪ 3/4" X 1 1/4" X 11'FT.
SHEAR RAIL ON OUTSIDE (2)

3/4" X 5 1/2" X 13"
CORNER KNEE (2)

(1 X 3" CROSS BEAM
USED UNDER SEAT
IF STRUT BELLIES IT)

⑨ 3/4" X 2" X 12"
SEAT CLEAT (4)

⑩ 3/4"X 6" X 7 3/4"
CENTER STRUT

④ 3/4" X 3" X 9 FT. 10"
INNER KEEL

② 3/8" X 12" X 11 FT.
PLYWOOD SIDES (2)

③ 2" X 2" X 12 1/2"
STEM BLOCK

HANK CLARK

⑫
3/4" X 1 1/4" X 10 1/2
OUTER STEM

⑤
3/4" X 1 1/2" X 9 FT. 9"
CHINE RAILS (2)

⑦ 3/4" X 1 1/8" X 9 FT. 10 1/2"
OUTER KEEL GOES ON LAST

⑥ 3/8" X 19 3/8" X 9 FT. 10 3/4" BOTTOM HALVES (2)

Inner stem joins two sides at the bow, as shown here. This is planed to a bevel for a good fit, then glued and screwed in place. Get the stem absolutely vertical to avoid nose that is askew.

With the front bow aligned and drilled, glue and screw it closed, as described. Note that two chine rails with planed bevels are now ready to be wedged into place. Study the diagrams for details.

With inner keel secured to side panels, front end glued and screwed, chine rails are then bent in (as shown here), ready for securing to interior sides; the 3/16-inch exposure is to be planed.

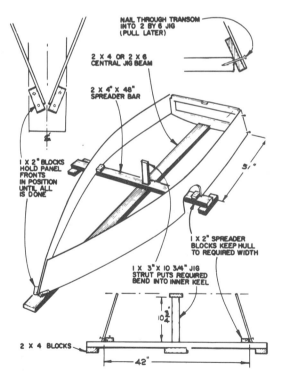

NAIL THROUGH TRANSOM INTO 2 BY 6 JIG (PULL LATER)

2 X 4 OR 2 X 6 CENTRAL JIG BEAM

2 X 4" X 48" SPREADER BAR

1 X 2" BLOCKS HOLD PANEL FRONTS IN POSITION UNTIL ALL IS DONE

5"

1 X 2" SPREADER BLOCKS KEEP HULL TO REQUIRED WIDTH

1 X 3" X 10 3/4" JIG STRUT PUTS REQUIRED BEND INTO INNER KEEL

2 X 4 BLOCKS

42"

Chine goes into notch cut for it in transom. Note the two screws joining the inner keel to transom.

With ¾-inch No. 7 Screwmate, predrill all holes for all panels two inches apart, as shown in photo.

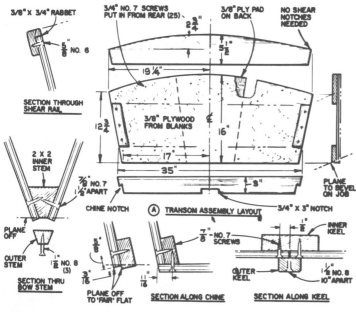

Diagram at left shows stern assembly details. Diagram below shows how to cut the panels from plywood.

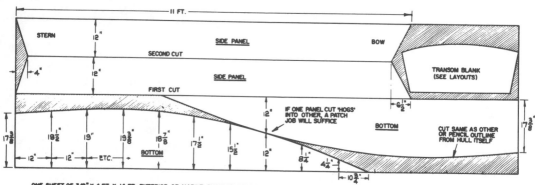

ONE SHEET OF 3/8" X 4 FT. X 14 FT. EXTERIOR OR MARINE PLYWOOD YIELDS ALL PANELS FOR COMPLETE ROWBOAT

Ratchet screwdriver makes short work of setting the screws; no linen strips are used on the glued side joint since chine face is milled at factory.

The final job before the bottom goes on is that of checking the planing job with a "fairing" stick, which measures flatness for installing the bottom.

Stanley's Surform tool, with its many small chisels, makes baby-skin smooth surfaces, is ideal for job.

Weldwood mix is brushed on at this point. Note that half of bottom is already secured in place.

Schedule for screwing the hull is shown in diagram at right.

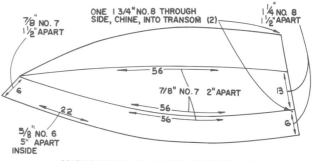

SCREW SCHEDULE ON PLANKING (ONE HALF TOTAL)

Linen strips are laid into Weldwood glue before securing bottom. Again compress glue onto surface.

To strengthen hull, cover exposed bottom side joint with a strip of lumber for chafing guard.

Outer keel goes on last, covers any gap between bottom halves, seals bottom, good launching skid.

The final touch for the nose is the outer stem It will be planed to a taper after screwed into place.

Seats are now screwed to cleats placed on sides with glue. Screws are driven in from the outside.

Sheer rail is rabbeted to mount atop side panels, serving as frame plus rib rail. Screw holds batten.

Rest of sheer rail is secured from inside every six inches. Note how side panels fit flush into rabbet.

Before painting boat, apply two coats of Firzite which seals outer plys, is solid base for paint job.

Final result of all your effort will be this fast moving, highly attractive rowboat, shown here with motor.

FOO-LING

By Hal Kelly

Build this class "A" or "B" runabout.

DRIVER got her to 45 mph and she is riding light for "A" despite his 170-pound weight.

FOO-LING will qualify under the A.P.B.A. rules for both "A" and "B" Stock Runabout and is very fast in both rough and good water. Highly maneuverable, she will bank in a tight turn right up on her side due to the fact that the upper chine is placed on the OUTSIDE of the non-trip which keeps the boat from sliding out. This type of construction I have never seen attempted on a plywood-planked hull. On a wider turn she can be made to ride the outside chine. As a marathon boat she is great. This strip of wood on the outside of her non-trip keeps her from diving into a big wave without offering a great deal of wind resistance. She rides beautifully when going into a headwind, won't wander all over the course, and runs as straight as an arrow. She will take any motor from 7 to 25 hp, but for motors other than the Champ Hot Rod and Mercury Quicksilver units, the transom will have to be made 17 inches high. Check with dealer for height.

Most important is getting the proper propeller for your outfit. This must be done before you try any hopping up of the motor. If you will give me the motor make, year, hp, and model number, and the weight of the boat with passengers, and what use you want to put your outfit to, I will tell you the make and kind of propeller you should use.

When building FOO-LING, please stick to the materials listed. With Fiberglas bottom all hardware and cushions she will weigh under 130 lbs. If you use Fiberglas on the bottom, you can use fir plywood—so what you save on plywood you can put into Fiberglas. With Fiberglas and all hardware she should cost about $180.00 and take about 80 hours to build.

After accumulatng the stock listed in the bill of materials, you are ready to start on the ribs. Full sized rib drawings are available. Due to space limitations only half of the ribs are shown, but since the ribs are the same on both sides this will offer no problem. Cut out all of your rib components and place them on the full-size rib drawings using Anchorfast nails and screws as indicated on the drawing. A piece of thin tracing or wax paper will keep the glue off your plans.

The bottom of each frame is continuous from chine to chine; check drawing for size and shape. The sides of the frames are 1½ inches wide and straight-sided; the large gussets form the non-trip chines. Place the frame components on the layout and hold them in place with temporary fastenings. Place two plywood gussets over frames (one on each side) and fasten with glue and ¾-inch No. 16 Anchorfast nails. You will not have to drill pilot holes for this size nail. Use as many and about the same placement as illustrated on your full size rib drawings. When all 4 gussets are in place, carefully inscribe the center line on both sides.

Assemble the transom and transom frame. Cut transom from ¼-inch thick plywood. Transom framing is $\frac{13}{16}$ inch or ⅞ inch thick. Assemble transom frame. All lapped joints should fit snugly. Coat mating surfaces of the joints and fasten together with ⅞-inch No. 8 screws. Carefully notch for battens, keel, bottom chine, and sheer

before assembling transom frame to transom. Glue and fasten transom to transom frame with ¾-inch No. 16 Anchorfast nails placed about two inches apart.

The keel and stem are one piece, ½x1½ inches, but forward of Rib No. 1 it is backed by another piece ½x1½ inches. Both are glued together when the proper shape has been obtained, and steaming is not necessary. This can be done now or later on, when all the ribs are set up.

After the glue in the frames has hardened, cut the notches for the bottom chine and sheer. Note that only in Rib No. 2 do the bottom stringers go through, on transom, Rib No. 3 and Rib No. 1 they butt.

The boat should be built on a level wooden floor, or on a wooden cradle laid on a concrete floor (see step-by-step drawings) in an area about the size of a one-car garage. Lay out the center line and frame lines on the floor or cradle according to the spacings given in the drawing, using such temporary bracing as you feel necessary. Set up frames and transom; a couple of nails will hold each frame to floor or cradle. When all is securely erected, double check and make sure everything lines up. Remember, no hooks or rockers in the bottom. Coat the bottom stringers and notches with glue and slip into place. Then fasten to ribs and transom with small blocks; glue and fasten in place with

YOU don't have to use this type of jig. The one illustrated on page 118 is adequate.

TRANSOM with afterplane in place. Two drain holes proved ideal for marathons.

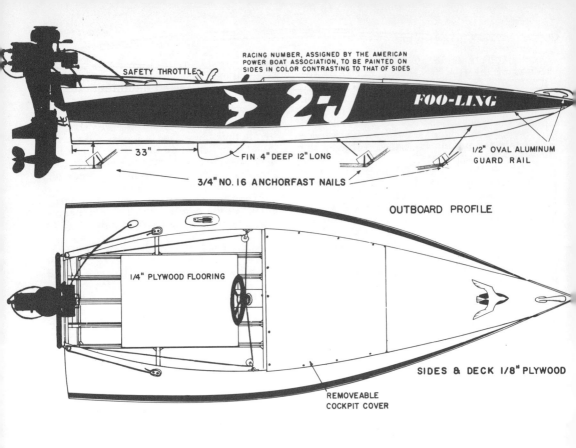

SAFETY THROTTLE

RACING NUMBER, ASSIGNED BY THE AMERICAN POWER BOAT ASSOCIATION, TO BE PAINTED ON SIDES IN COLOR CONTRASTING TO THAT OF SIDES

2-J   FOO-LING

33"

FIN 4" DEEP 12" LONG

1/2" OVAL ALUMINUM GUARD RAIL

3/4" NO.16 ANCHORFAST NAILS

OUTBOARD PROFILE

1/4" PLYWOOD FLOORING

SIDES & DECK 1/8" PLYWOOD

REMOVEABLE COCKPIT COVER

1-inch No. 16 steel brads. Next slip the keel in place with glue and 1¼-inch No. 8 flathead wood screws, using two screws to secure to transom and all ribs, and one about every 8 inches to the bottom stringer. The same procedure is used on all battens except that one screw is used to fasten to transom and all ribs. Next secure the bottom chine and sheers, using glue and 1½-inch No. 8 flathead wood screws. Where they butt against the stem and transom, bevel them to obtain a good landing; one screw at each frame, transom and stem. The bottom chine is cut thinner (⅝ inch thick) from the bow to Rib No. 1, where it gradually takes on its original thickness; this will allow it to bend easier and lighten the nose. Don't forget fin bracing from Rib No. 2 to Rib No. 3. Add 1 inch after plane to transom.

Fairing is probably one of the most important phases. If you have done a good job of setting up the frames, this should not be too difficult a task. Use a plane and a good wood file. Carefully trim and fair

so the plywood planking will lie on all structural members. Check the fair from time to time as you progress by springing battens around the structure. Remember that from Rib No. 2 to the transom the bottom must be perfectly flat, and the plywood bottom can't be flat unless the structural members are faired flat. The non-trip chines are fitted first. A large sheet of wrapping paper will come in handy to give you a rough idea of their shape. Cut the panels a bit oversize, clamp in place and mark the outline of the bottom chine. Remove them and cut out a wee bit over size. Remember to glue and fasten in place the ⅛-inch thick by 1¼-inch square wood blocks at the top of the non-trip chine of each rib. The bottom goes over the edge of the chine except up toward the front where they butt each other. After the non-trip chine is fitted, glue and fasten it in place using ¾-inch No. 16 Anchorfast nails to transom, bottom chine and stem, and one nail at the top edge of the chine at the transom and each rib.

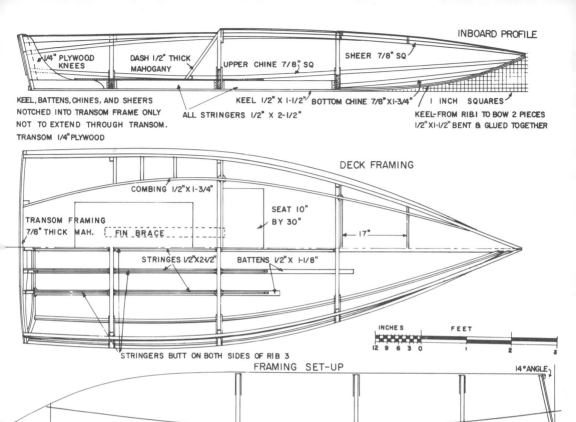

1/4" PLYWOOD KNEES

DASH 1/2" THICK MAHOGANY

UPPER CHINE 7/8" SQ

SHEER 7/8" SQ

KEEL, BATTENS, CHINES, AND SHEERS NOTCHED INTO TRANSOM FRAME ONLY NOT TO EXTEND THROUGH TRANSOM. TRANSOM 1/4" PLYWOOD

KEEL 1/2" X 1-1/2" BOTTOM CHINE 7/8"X1-3/4"

ALL STRINGERS 1/2" X 2-1/2"

I INCH SQUARES

KEEL-FROM RIB.1 TO BOW 2 PIECES 1/2" X1-1/2" BENT & GLUED TOGETHER

DECK FRAMING

COMBING 1/2"X 1-3/4"

SEAT 10" BY 30"

TRANSOM FRAMING 7/8" THICK MAH. FIN BRACE

17"

STRINGES 1/2"X2-1/2" BATTENS 1/2"X 1-1/8"

INCHES   FEET

12 9 6 3 0   1   2   3

STRINGERS BUTT ON BOTH SIDES OF RIB 3

FRAMING SET-UP

14°ANGLE

FLOOR LINE

RIB 1   RIB 2   RIB 3   TRANSOM

48"   32"   28"   24"

You will have to fair the bottom of the non-trip where the bottom will rest on it, and up toward the front where the bottom butts the chine. The bottom goes on much the same way and is all one piece with a V cut in the front to allow the bottom to come to a V. Up toward the front it will take a little careful fitting to make the bottom butt into the non-trip chine. Use a few screws to temporarily hold the bottom in place while you are fitting it. Mark on the bottom from the inside where all the battens, etc., come in contact.

Glue is applied to all structural members that the bottom will touch, and also to the bottom where you have marked areas the battens, etc., will contact. Put the bottom in place (a two-man job) and screw in the same screws that held it temporarily in place while you were fitting the bottom. Three-fourth-inch No. 16 Anchorfast nails are used to fasten the bottom to the transom, keel, battens and stem. Place about every 1¾ inches apart and countersink a bit (about $\frac{1}{16}$ inch). The bottom is best

fastened to the battens forward of Rib No. 2 with ⅝-inch No. 8 flathead wood screws, placed about every 4 inches apart, and countersink about $\frac{1}{16}$ inch. After the bottom is dry, plane the edge at the same angle as the chine, except toward the back where it is allowed to remain square. This gives you a little lip to help grip the water on turns.

The upper chine is now fastened in place. This is ⅞ inch square and starts to taper toward the front to nothing at the very front. This taper starts about 5 feet from the front. Glue and 1½-inch No. 8 flathead wood screws are used to fasten the upper chine to all ribs and transom, well countersunk. From the inside the non-trip is fastened to the upper chine with ¾-inch No. 16 Anchorfast nails set 1¾ inches apart. At the very front this upper chine is best clamped in place until the glue is dry. At this point take the boat off the floor or jig and set it up on two well-padded horses at a good workable height. Saw off the extra piece on transom and ribs.

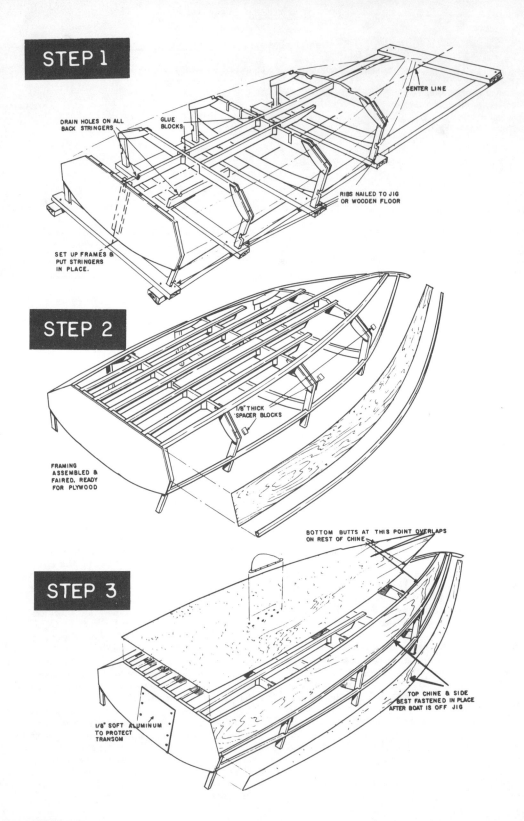

STEP 1

CENTER LINE

DRAIN HOLES ON ALL
BACK STRINGERS

GLUE
BLOCKS

RIBS NAILED TO JIG
OR WOODEN FLOOR

SET UP FRAMES &
PUT STRINGERS
IN PLACE.

STEP 2

1/8" THICK
SPACER BLOCKS

FRAMING
ASSEMBLED &
FAIRED, READY
FOR PLYWOOD

BOTTOM BUTTS AT THIS POINT OVERLAPS
ON REST OF CHINE

STEP 3

TOP CHINE & SIDE
BEST FASTENED IN PLACE
AFTER BOAT IS OFF JIG

1/8" SOFT ALUMINUM
TO PROTECT
TRANSOM

NON-TRIP chines in place and ready for bottom planking, which is in one piece.

TRANSOM with all bracing in place. Varnish the inside at this time, give 4 coats.

Fashion the deck beam, cockpit coaming, and other braces according to the plan; all are ½ inch thick. The cockpit coaming runs from 3½ inches wide at the transom to ¾ inch wide where it is fastened to the inside of the sheer. Fit transom bracing and knees in place as indicated in drawings and photos. Knees are glued and fastened to the stringers and transom bracing with Anchorfast nails and screws. If you use a flush throttle, now is the time to put in the bracing for it.

Now fair off the upper chine and fit it to the sides. The side is glued and fastened in place with ¾-inch No. 16 Anchorfast nails spaced 1¾ inches apart. When the side is dry, fair off at the upper chine as shown in the full size Rib Drawings; also fair at the sheer line. The side decking is glued and fastened in place with ¾-inch No. 16 Anchorfast nails. The deck beam on Rib No. 1 is built up on one side so you can slip the removable cockpit cover in place after the front middle decking is fastened in place. Front middle decking is fastened in place in the same way as the side decking. Glue and fasten flooring in place with ¾-inch No. 16 Anchorfast nails. This forms a structural part of the bottom and will prevent it from warping or cupping.

The front seat offers no problem and is not glued in place. Use ⅞-inch No. 8 flathead wood screws. Sand the entire boat down and varnish or paint to suit your taste. Remember to varnish under the floor boards BEFORE you fasten them in place. Also, it is a good idea to varnish the entire inside before the decking is put in place. Give the inside 4 coats. The bottom, to the top of the non-trip chine, is fiberglass. Read fiberglassing instructions on page 68. Now screw fin in place and install hardware. I bolt my back lifting handles in place as I use them to tie down my motor.

Now for that first test run! If you are racing, be sure to have a good, sound, safe helmet. Always wear it and a good life jacket with collar, even when testing. Motor angle and height are very important for racing and a motor ⅛ inch too high or low has lost many a race. A marine speedometer is handy to have while making these adjustments. Spend a little time with your outfit; learn how to handle her; get the feel; find out where the best place is to kneel in her when turning, both in calm and rough water. The first turn in a race is no place to learn the feel of your boat. Remember, you have a great boat, but it is only as good as the driver.

BILL OF MATERIALS

BRONZE, MONEL or EVERDUR FASTENINGS
2 dozen ⅝" #8 flathead wood screws
1 gross of ⅞" #8 flathead wood screws
2 gross of 1¼" #8 flathead wood screws
4 dozen of 1½" #8 flathead wood screws
3 lbs. of 1" #16 Anchorfast nails 950 to lb.
8 carriage bolts ¼" x 4" with nuts and washers

PAINT PRODUCTS
5 lbs. of Weldwood glue
1 lb. of Wood Dough or similar surface filler
1 gal. of Spar varnish for interior, decking, and exterior

PLYWOOD
Decking and sides 2 sheets of marine grade plywood ⅛" x 4' x 8'
Bottom non-trip chines, seat, and flooring 2 sheets of Marine grade Plywood ¼" x 4' x 12'

SITKA SPRUCE or WHITE CEDAR
Sheers and upper chine .. 4 pieces ⅞" sq. x 12'
Battens ....4 pieces ½" x 1⅛" x 8'
Keel .... 1 piece ½" x 1½" x 12'

Bottom stringer ....1 piece ½" x 2½" x 8'
Bottom stringers .... 4 pieces ½" x 2½" x 7'
Frames .... 1 piece ⅞" x 12" x 12'
Deck frames, etc. .... 1 piece ½" x 8" x 12'

HONDURAS MAHOGANY
Inside of keel at bow .... 1 piece ½" x 1½" x 5'
Transom framing .... 1 piece ⅞" x 8" x 16'
Bottom chine .... 2 pieces ⅞" x 1¾" x 12'
Dash and dash beam ......1 piece ½" x 7" x 7'

HARDWARE
1 Steering wheel
1 piece of steering rope 26'
1 Safety throttle
1 Bowden throttle cable 5' long
1 Racing fin
2 Forward steering pulleys, with anchor straps
2 Rear pulleys
2 Steering line tieback
2 Stern lifting handles
1 Bow handle
24' of ½" oval aluminum
2 Steel 'S' hooks to hold rope block to steering bar

FIBERGLAS

The bottom of FOO-LING is Fiberglased, up to the top of the non-trip chine at the expense of 10 extra lbs. Costs ran me a little less than 40 cents a foot. I used a medium weight glasscolth, 50" wide, which left no seam on the bottom at all. A thin application of the plastic was applied to the bare wood with a brush. After it had hardened (the next day), I laid the cloth over the bottom and trimmed to fit. You need not cut out a V for the front as it drapes over the bow very well. A generous coat of plastic was applied to the bottom, the cloth laid over the bottom and smoothed out, and more plastic was applied with a squeegee to smooth. The cloth becomes almost invisible if applied correctly. The next day with a grinder I carefully ground down the surface so that it was smooth, flat, and even, and one more coat was applied with a brush, and carefully smoothed with a lot of elbow grease and wet sandpaper. Then a lacquer compound was used to give a plate-glass finish. Fiberglas is composed of a plastic and a hardener plus the glass cloth or mats. You have to work rather fast. It's a two man job as the "pot life" is short or long depending on how much hardener you use. By short "pot life" I mean that the mixture hardens in the pot before it hardens on the boat. One minute it is liquid, but then it starts to turn into a jelly and proceeds to get very hard in a matter of seconds. I would say that for the beginner it is a dog job. But the results are very rewarding. It is literally as tough as glass and just as smooth. This is not intended to be a full discussion by any means, but just a few words to let you know what you are in for if you would like to Fiberglas the bottom.

Some say it's luck that often wins a race, but you will note that the best drivers make their own luck. You have a good boat, but a well-tuned motor and the proper prop, plus good setup also help to win. Oh yes, and the driver counts, too—you know darn well he does.

To get your racing numbers for A.P.B.A. racing, write to the American Power Boat Association; The Whittier Hotel, 415 Burns Dr., Detroit, Mich. 48214.

A mistake many new drivers make is that in testing and adjusting their motor too early the day of the race—setting their motor for the best speed at that time. A few hours later their race comes up, and perhaps by now, a strong wind has roughened the water so that in the middle of the race they find they are much too high or kicked out too much.

It's always nice to test out on good water; it's nice riding and you go much faster.

FIBERGLAS cloth cut to size. Notice how well it drapes over stem without cutting a V.

ALL SET up and ready to run. Note aluminum plate under motor to protect transom.

But I make it a point to do at least half of my testing on rough water. Try setting up some buoys and practice turns. I know a few fellows who set up their own course and practice out on it as if they were running a race; they even have a starting clock to practice on. I'll admit that there's nothing like an actual race for experience, but testing will be a big help.

Motor setup is not easy to learn. It's hard to know whether to kick it in (for rough water) or out (for calm water) or how high to run. You can look around and see how the better drivers are running their boats, but frankly this is of little help because boats and driving styles differ. I have seen two good drivers at a race both running the same make hydro, motor, and prop: one ran on the fourth motor notch, the other on the third. Both took a first and a second, and were tied on time. I'm sure this would confuse any beginner. When you practice for a race, don't just run around. Try all kind of setups.

Pickup means a lot in short-course racing and I often sacrifice a few miles of top speed for acceleration. As an example, before one race a friend of mine was passing me on a long stretch down the river. He was running faster than anyone else. With a beautiful start he hit the first buoy first in a three-buoy turn, but coming out of the turn five fellows passed him and I think he finally finished a sad sixth. I managed to steal a second in that heat.

The main thing you can do to a stock motor and remain legal is to carefully set up your reed cage and points. Run the exact amount of oil in your motor that the manufacturer recommends—no more, no less. In breaking a new motor don't run a rich oil mixture, but set your high speed jet a little richer for the first hour, with the spark on two-thirds. Run the motor at half-throttle for 15 minutes. Then give the motor a five-minute break and run again for 15 minutes. Do this for about one hour running time. Now take her out and boot it wide open for a stretch, but for the next two hours running time refrain from any continuous high speed runs.

I always run my motor with a full butterfly. In case of a flip it's much safer for you and the other drivers, and will save you from a blown motor.

All in all it's a great sport and I never met a finer group of people than those within the sport. We cover about 8,000 miles each year just going to the races. When I go, the whole family goes: wife, two kids and the dog. Win, lose, or draw, we all have a picnic. See you at the races. •

LARGE SCALE PLANS

with full rib drawings (plus six colorful decals) are available for building this boat. They are $12.00 post paid. Order from Hal Kelly's Plans, P. O. Box 1767, Fort Pierce, Florida 33450. Specify Plan FB-FOO-LING.

MALAHINI

By Glen L. Witt, N.A.

A 16-foot outboard runabout with generous beam.

MODERN STYLING, a deep vee and a wide beam give Malahini dry, safe characteristics.

A GENEROUS SIZE outboard runabout is the Malahini, 15 feet 11 inches in overall length, with an extreme beam of 6 feet 7 inches. She is a particularly versatile boat with the seats being of the floating type. That is, they may readily be removed, providing a flat area 9 feet long, and up to 5 feet 9 inches wide for carrying camping gear. The aft seat could be turned around and placed back to back with the front seat for trolling or for a water ski observer.

The generous vee in the fore portion, and the wide beam, make for a dry, safe boat. The construction is rugged, and intended to "take it." The self-bailing motor well prevents any sudden wave or backwash from entering the boat.

All lumber used should be first-grade white oak, dark red Philippine mahogany, or Sitka spruce. All plywood must be intended for marine or exterior use. All joints throughout the construction should be glued with rescorcinol or urea-resin glue. All fastenings should be bronze, hot-dipped galvanized, or brass.

BUILDING INSTRUCTIONS

FRAMES: The frames are fabricated from 1-inch material: oak, mahogany, or spruce. The bottom and side frame members are joined with a ⅜-inch plywood gusset on either side of the frames. The bottom frame members at No. 1, No. 2, and No. 3 are in single width from chine to chine. The frame at No. 4 has the two half frame members joined together by a floor timber of the same material as the frame. The plywood gussets are assembled to the

frames with glue, and nailed with annular thread type nails. The floor timber on No. 4 is assembled with a minimum of five 1½-inch No. 8 screws per member. The notches for the various members may be cut after frame assembly.

TRANSOM: The ¾-inch plywood transom is framed with 1-inch oak, mahogany, or spruce. All notches must be cut into the framing members before assembly to the plywood transom. In assembly, fasten the frame to the transom with 1½-inch No. 8 screws, spaced approximately 6 inches apart.

STEM: The stem is built up from two laminations of ¾-inch thick exterior plywood. In assembly, coat the mating surfaces liberally with glue, and fasten together with 1½-inch No. 8 screws, spaced a maximum of 6 inches apart.

BREASTHOOK AND CHINE BLOCKING: These members are built up from two layers of ¾-inch exterior plywood. The breasthook is used between the sheer clamps, and the chine blocking between the chines at the stem junction.

TRANSOM KNEE: The transom knee is fabricated from three laminations of ¾-inch plywood. In assembly, the knee bolts to the keel and transom with 5/16-inch carriage bolts.

BUILDING FORM: Details for the building form are given in the plans. Basically, the form consists of two longitudinal setup members that are level, both lengthwise and athwartships. These are supported on legs, the whole being anchored to the floor. The frames are

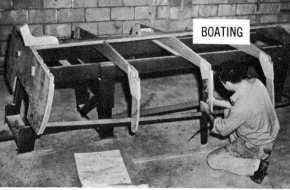

STEM, breasthook and chine block assembly is mounted to No. 4 frame. Note bolting.

PLUMB each frame on leveled building form, then brace to form to prevent movement.

CHINE members are fastened at stem, sprung about hull. Chine angles across blocking.

BEVEL chine with wood rasp at each frame for easy fairing. Follow contour of frame.

mounted bottom side up on the form, spaced per the dimensions shown, and accurately centered with a chalk line. The transom may be located by the use of the knee bolted to the keel. The height of the breasthook-stem assembly is carefully blocked to the dimension noted.

KEEL: The keel is a 1x4-inch member of oak, mahogany or spruce, laminated on the inside with ⅜-inch plywood. The keel is fitted into notches at the frame and transom, and fastened to them with 2-inch No. 10 screws.

CHINE LOG: The junction of the side planking and bottom planking is called the chine point, and the backing member is the chine log. This member is full length 1x2-inch oak or spruce. Fit into the frame notches, coat with glue, and fasten with 2-inch No. 10 screws.

SHEER CLAMP: The junction for the side planking and decking is the sheer, and the backing member is called the sheer clamp. Sheer clamps are built up from two laminations of ⅝x1¼-inch mahogany or spruce. The first layer is sprung around the hull, followed by the second layer, liberally coating the initial one with glue.

FAIRING: All of the members; sheer clamp, chine, keel, stem, and transom must be beveled or faired to allow the planking to lay flat on all areas. Care should be taken in the after section of the hull to assure that the running lines are true and straight. While fairing, always stand back from the hull and sight across the lines, to eliminate any humps or bumps in the fairing process.

BOTTOM BATTENS: The bottom 1x2-inch oak or mahogany battens are notched into each frame and the transom. They are located as noted per the drawings, and anchored in place with 2-inch No. 10 screws.

LIMBERS: Limber holes, to allow all bilge water to drain aft, should be notched on the outboard side of all longitudinals.

SIDE PLANKING: The ¼-inch side planking should be in full length. Shorter panels can be used, butt joined per the details. Lean the plywood panel against the side of the hull, and scribe around its extremities. Remove the panel and cut roughly to shape with a fine-tooth saw. The portion that will butt join with the bottom planking from approximately frame No. 4

BILL OF MATERIALS

OAK, MAHOGANY OR SPRUCE
Frames, transom—40 random bd. ft.,
  1" stock
Keel—1 piece 1"x4"x13'
Battens—2 pieces 1"x2"x12'
        2 pieces 1"x2"x10'
Chine log—2 pieces 1"x2"x18'
Sheer clamp—4 pieces 5/8"x1 1/4"x18'
Intermediate deck beam—1 piece
  1"x4"x5'
Deck battens—2 pieces 1"x2"x5'
Strongback—1 piece 1"x3"x6'
Motor well longitudinals—2 pieces
  1"x4"x3 1/2'
Aft well deck beam—1 piece 1"x6"x3'
Blocking, cleats—as required
Floorboard battens—2 pieces 1"x2"x9'

D. F. PLYWOOD AB, EXT.
Frame gussets, keel laminations—1 piece
  3/8"x4'x8'
Transom, stem, chine blocking,
  breasthook—1 piece 3/4"x4'x8'
Floorboards, seats—3 pieces 3/8"x4'x9'
Seat brackets—1 piece 3/4"x4'x6'

MAHOGANY FACED PLYWOOD EXT. AA
Decking—2 pieces 1/4"x4'x8'

D. F. PLYWOOD AA MARINE
Planking, side—2 pieces 1/4"x3'x18'
Planking, bottom—2 pieces 3/8"x3'x16'

MAHOGANY
Carlings—2 pieces 1/2"x4"x9'
Dash—1 piece 1"x7"x6'
Lower bumper rail—2 pieces 1"x4"x7'

MISCELLANEOUS
Motor well brace—1 piece D. F. 2"x4"x3'
Motor well plywood—cut from scraps
  of planking

FASTENINGS
Screws: flat head, wood, bronze or
  hot dipped galvanized.
  3/4"   # 8—3 gross
  1"   # 8—4 gross
  1 1/4" # 8—1 gross
  1 1/2" # 8—1 gross
  2"   #10—1 gross
  3"   #14—3 dozen
Carriage bolts: complete w. nuts,
  washers, bronze or hot dipped
  galvanized.
  5/16"x4" —4 required
  5/16"x7" —2 required
  1/4"x2 1/4" —2 required
Nails: annular ring type, bronze
  or monel   1" —2 lbs.   1 1/4"—1 lb.

Glue: plastic resin type Weldwood or
  comparable volume Rescorinol
  type—10 lbs.

forward, must be fitted along the chine. The balance may be left long for subsequent trimming. Fasten the planking to all members, per the directions given in the fastening schedule.

BOTTOM PLANKING: The planking for the bottom is optionally 1/4-inch or 3/8-inch plywood. For the rougher usage, the 3/8 inch in full length is recommended. Fit the bottom planking carefully along the part that will butt join with the side planking. Aft of this point, the bottom planking will lap the side planking to be planed off after installation. Fasten per the fastening schedule.

OUTER KEEL: The outer keel of 1-inch oak, mahogany or spruce is fastened over the joint of the bottom planking.

FIBERGLASSING: The fiberglassing of any fir plywood hull is a distinct advantage to prevent checking so common with fir plywood. A complete fiberglassing kit can be obtained from Glen L for covering the bottom only or for covering the bottom, sides, and transom. These kits provide complete material for the job including brushes, squeegee, acetone, resin, cloth, etc.

SPRAY RAIL: The 1x1 1/4-inch spray rail covers the junction of the side and bottom planking, and is fastened with 2-inch No. 10 screws, spaced 12 inches apart.

INTERMEDIATE DECK BEAM: The intermediate deck beam is installed as shown in the drawings, cut from 1-inch mahogany to the same crown as frame No.

FASTEN panel by clamping along chine at transom. Attach along chine line first.

BOTTOM panel clamped along centerline of stem. Attach forward from transition point.

TRANSOM

TRANSOM IS CUT FROM 3/4" PLYWOOD - FRAMED WITH 1" OAK OR MAHOGANY

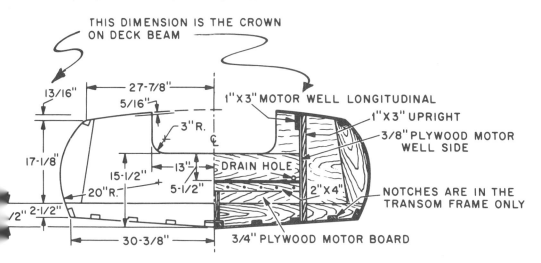

THIS DIMENSION IS THE CROWN ON DECK BEAM

13/16"
27-7/8"
5/16"
1"X3" MOTOR WELL LONGITUDINAL
3"R.
1"X3" UPRIGHT
3/8" PLYWOOD MOTOR WELL SIDE
17-1/8"
13"
DRAIN HOLE
15-1/2"
20"R.
5-1/2"
2"X4"
NOTCHES ARE IN THE TRANSOM FRAME ONLY
/2" 2-1/2"
30-3/8"
3/4" PLYWOOD MOTOR BOARD

FRAME   NO. 1

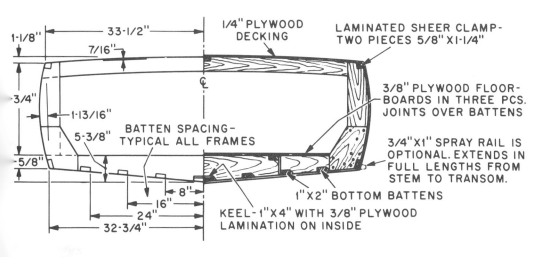

1-1/8"
33-1/2"
1/4" PLYWOOD DECKING
LAMINATED SHEER CLAMP- TWO PIECES 5/8" X1-1/4"
7/16"
3/4"
3/8" PLYWOOD FLOOR- BOARDS IN THREE PCS. JOINTS OVER BATTENS
1-13/16"
5-3/8"
BATTEN SPACING- TYPICAL ALL FRAMES
3/4"X1" SPRAY RAIL IS OPTIONAL. EXTENDS IN FULL LENGTHS FROM STEM TO TRANSOM.
-5/8"
8"
1"X2" BOTTOM BATTENS
16"
24"
KEEL-1"X4" WITH 3/8" PLYWOOD LAMINATION ON INSIDE
32-3/4"

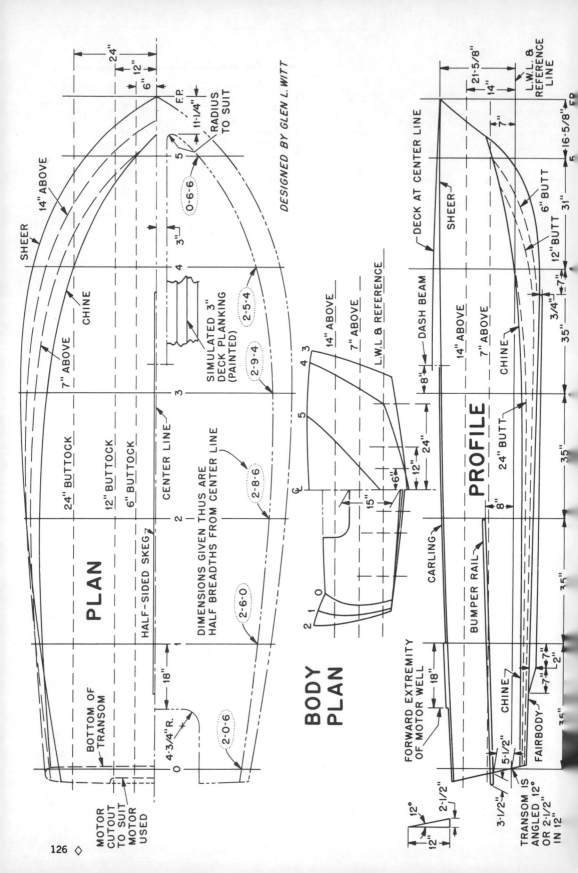

DESIGNED BY GLEN L. WITT

PLAN

HALF-SIDED SKEG

DIMENSIONS GIVEN THUS ARE
HALF BREADTHS FROM CENTER LINE

SIMULATED 3"
DECK PLANKING
(PAINTED)

SHEER

14" ABOVE

CHINE

7" ABOVE

24" BUTTOCK

12" BUTTOCK

6" BUTTOCK

CENTER LINE

BOTTOM OF TRANSOM

MOTOR CUTOUT TO SUIT MOTOR USED

4-3/4" R.

18"

11-1/4"

RADIUS TO SUIT

F.P.

0-6-6

3"

2-5-4

2-9-4

2-8-6

2-6-0

2-0-6

BODY PLAN

14" ABOVE

7" ABOVE

L.W.L. & REFERENCE

15"

12°

2-1/2"

12"

PROFILE

DECK AT CENTER LINE

SHEER

DASH BEAM

CARLING

BUMPER RAIL

FORWARD EXTREMITY OF MOTOR WELL

14" ABOVE

7" ABOVE

CHINE

24" BUTT

8"

18"

CHINE

FAIRBODY

TRANSOM IS ANGLED 12°
OR 2-1/2" IN 12"

5-1/2"

3-1/2"

7"

7"

2"

L.W.L. & REFERENCE LINE

21-5/8"

14"

7"

6" BUTT

12" BUTT

16-5/8"

31"

35"

35"

3/4"

3.5"

3.5"

8"

12"

24"

6"

126 ◇

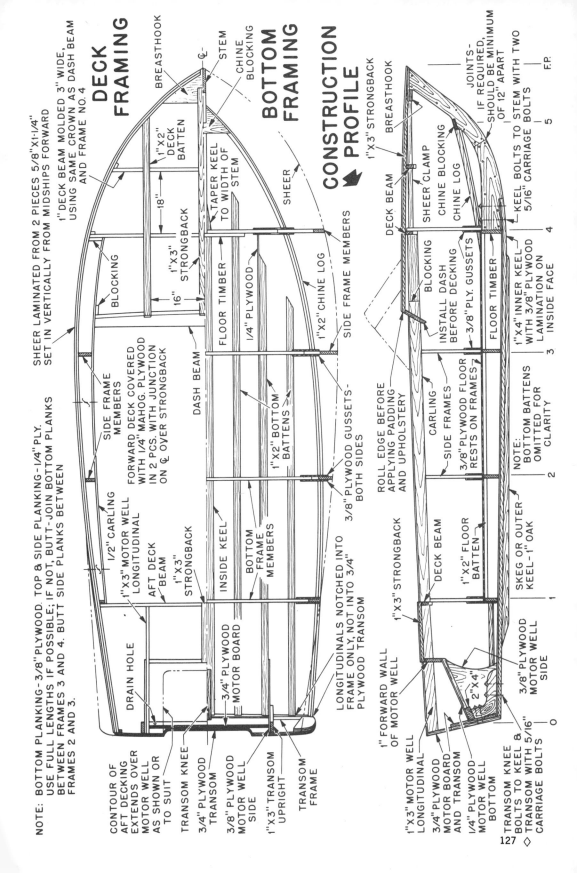

DECK FRAMING

BOTTOM FRAMING

CONSTRUCTION PROFILE ➤

NOTE: BOTTOM PLANKING-3/8" PLYWOOD. TOP & SIDE PLANKING-1/4" PLY. USE FULL LENGTHS IF POSSIBLE; IF NOT, BUTT-JOIN BOTTOM PLANKS BETWEEN FRAMES 3 AND 4. BUTT SIDE PLANKS BETWEEN FRAMES 2 AND 3.

SHEER LAMINATED FROM 2 PIECES 5/8"X1-1/4" SET IN VERTICALLY FROM MIDSHIPS FORWARD

1" DECK BEAM MOLDED 3" WIDE, USING SAME CROWN AS DASH BEAM AND FRAME NO. 4

BREASTHOOK

STEM

CHINE BLOCKING

1"x2" DECK BATTEN

18"

1"x3" STRONGBACK

TAPER KEEL TO WIDTH OF STEM

SHEER

BLOCKING

16"

1"x3" STRONGBACK

FLOOR TIMBER

1/4" PLYWOOD

1"x2" CHINE LOG

SIDE FRAME MEMBERS

DASH BEAM

SIDE FRAME MEMBERS

FORWARD DECK COVERED WITH 1/4" MAHOG. PLYWOOD IN 2 PCS. WITH JUNCTION ON ℄ OVER STRONGBACK

1"x2" BOTTOM BATTENS

3/8" PLYWOOD GUSSETS- BOTH SIDES

1/2" CARLING

AFT DECK BEAM

1"x3" STRONGBACK

INSIDE KEEL

BOTTOM FRAME MEMBERS

LONGITUDINALS NOTCHED INTO FRAME ONLY, NOT INTO 3/4" PLYWOOD TRANSOM

CONTOUR OF AFT DECKING EXTENDS OVER MOTOR WELL AS SHOWN OR TO SUIT

DRAIN HOLE

TRANSOM KNEE

3/4" PLYWOOD MOTOR BOARD

3/8" PLYWOOD MOTOR WELL SIDE

1"x3" TRANSOM UPRIGHT

TRANSOM FRAME

1"x3" STRONGBACK

BREASTHOOK

SHEER CLAMP

CHINE BLOCKING

CHINE LOG

JOINTS- IF REQUIRED, SHOULD BE MINIMUM OF 12" APART

KEEL BOLTS TO STEM WITH TWO 3/8" PLYWOOD 5/16" CARRIAGE BOLTS

F.P.

5

DECK BEAM

BLOCKING

INSTALL DASH BEFORE DECKING

CARLING

SIDE FRAMES

3/8" PLY. GUSSETS

FLOOR TIMBER

1"x4" INNER KEEL WITH 3/8" PLYWOOD LAMINATION ON INSIDE FACE

4

3

ROLL EDGE BEFORE APPLYING PADDING AND UPHOLSTERY

3/8" PLYWOOD FLOOR RESTS ON FRAMES

NOTE: BOTTOM BATTENS OMITTED FOR CLARITY

2

1"x3" STRONGBACK

DECK BEAM

1"x2" FLOOR BATTEN

SKEG OR OUTER KEEL-1" OAK

1

1" FORWARD WALL OF MOTOR WELL

1"x3" MOTOR WELL LONGITUDINAL

3/4" PLYWOOD MOTOR BOARD AND TRANSOM

1/4" PLYWOOD MOTOR WELL BOTTOM

TRANSOM KNEE BOLTS TO KEEL & TRANSOM WITH 5/16" CARRIAGE BOLTS

2"x4"

3/8" PLYWOOD MOTOR WELL SIDE

0

FRAME NO. 2

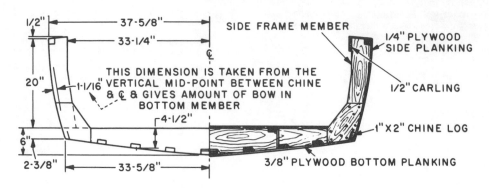

1/2"
37-5/8"
33-1/4"
SIDE FRAME MEMBER
1/4" PLYWOOD SIDE PLANKING
THIS DIMENSION IS TAKEN FROM THE VERTICAL MID-POINT BETWEEN CHINE & ℄ & GIVES AMOUNT OF BOW IN BOTTOM MEMBER
20"
1-1/16"
1/2" CARLING
4-1/2"
6"
1" X 2" CHINE LOG
2-3/8"
33-5/8"
3/8" PLYWOOD BOTTOM PLANKING

FRAME NO. 3

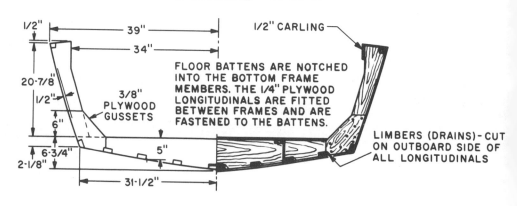

1/2"
39"
34"
1/2" CARLING
FLOOR BATTENS ARE NOTCHED INTO THE BOTTOM FRAME MEMBERS. THE 1/4" PLYWOOD LONGITUDINALS ARE FITTED BETWEEN FRAMES AND ARE FASTENED TO THE BATTENS.
20-7/8"
1/2"
3/8" PLYWOOD GUSSETS
6"
6-3/4"
5"
LIMBERS (DRAINS)-CUT ON OUTBOARD SIDE OF ALL LONGITUDINALS
2-1/8"
31-1/2"

FRAME NO. 4

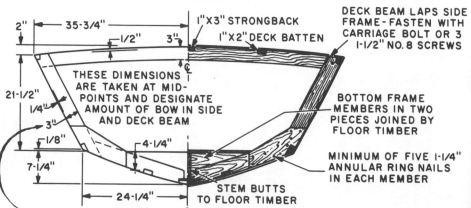

2"
35-3/4"
1" X 3" STRONGBACK
1/2"
3"
1" X 2" DECK BATTEN
DECK BEAM LAPS SIDE FRAME-FASTEN WITH CARRIAGE BOLT OR 3 1-1/2" NO. 8 SCREWS
THESE DIMENSIONS ARE TAKEN AT MID-POINTS AND DESIGNATE AMOUNT OF BOW IN SIDE AND DECK BEAM
21-1/2"
1/4"
3"
1/8"
BOTTOM FRAME MEMBERS IN TWO PIECES JOINED BY FLOOR TIMBER
4-1/4"
7-1/4"
MINIMUM OF FIVE 1-1/4" ANNULAR RING NAILS IN EACH MEMBER
24-1/4"
STEM BUTTS TO FLOOR TIMBER

MINIMUM OF 3" WIDTH ON BOTH- SIDES & BOTTOM MEMBERS AND DECK BEAMS- (TYPICAL OF ALL FRAMES)

4. Fasten to the blocking on the sheer, as indicated.

CARLING: The carling is the member that forms the longitudinal extremity of the cockpit area. This 1-inch mahogany member extends from the transom to the No. 4 deck beam.

DASH BEAM: The dash beam of 1-inch mahogany, cut at the same crown as frame No. 4, is fastened between the carlings with 2-inch No. 10 screws.

MOTOR WELL: The motor well is fabricated from ⅜-inch plywood sides that extend from the batten at the bottom of the boat to the decking longitudinal member, and is fastened to a 1x3-inch transom upright, as indicated. On top of the transom knee, a 2x4-inch Douglas fir brace is bolted to the transom with ¼-inch bolts.

STRONGBACK: The 1x3-inch strongback is located on the centerline of the boat, and is notched into each of the frames in each of the deck beams.

DECK BATTENS: The 1x2-inch mahogany or spruce deck battens are located per the drawings, and notched into the beams similarly to the strongback.

DECKING: The decking must be faired to allow the decking to mate to all members. Forward decking is ¼-inch mahogany-faced plywood. The decking should extend along the side decks as far as possible, from a 4x8-inch panel. At this point, it is joined to the side decking with a butt joint. Use a ⅜-inch butt block, extending 3 inches to 4 inches to the side of the joint. The decking is nailed in place per the fastening schedule. Before it is laid, the decking may be grooved to simulate planking with a power saw, table saw, or router.

FLOORBOARDS: The ⅜-inch floorboards are in three parts. They are fitted around the frames to provide a flush area in the cockpit, resting on battens notched into the frames.

SEATS: The seats are detailed in the drawings. These consist of ¾-inch plywood angle-brackets with ⅜-inch sides or ½-inch sides and bottoms.

STEERING AND CONTROLS: The steering and remote controls should be sent to the forward cockpit to suit the type of motor and controls used.

GAS TANK: The gasoline tank should be stored under the aft deck area. On the opposite side of the gasoline tank, the battery box should be mounted on a sheet of ⅜-inch plywood, and enclosed in a fiberglass box. •

BASIC framework of decking completed. Carling members, strongback battens in place.

BARNABY

by Henry Clark

Build this 16-foot cabin cruiser for under $500

THIS is it! For less than $500—$446 to be exact—I built this 16-foot cabin cruiser. Framing lumber for the hull costs $86; plywood planking $170; miscellaneous wood, screws and paint $100; control hardware $90; total cost for the hull, $446. Roomy but trailable; it's small enough to keep our lot uncluttered. It carries a slew of camping gear, plus my wife, three kids —and a dog! Yet it planes easily, just like a runabout. Good stability, sturdy oak framing, ⅜-inch plywood hull and mahogany trim for that "cruiser" look. The cabin sleeps two adults plus a child.

The wheel and controls in the cabin are for use in wet weather. They are coupled to the helm in the open cockpit for stand-up or sit-down steering. Portholes for Junior to watch the splash, a memory every boy should have—wide gunwales for walking—grab rails on the roof—windows that open for ventilation —an upper windshield to keep the wind off the skipper—fuel tanks under seats, which are hinged—seat back that lowers, for motor attention—a self-bailing water well to keep out following seas—a high freeboard to keep out spray. Barnaby's got 'em all!

I built her in three months' "spare" time, from Labor Day to Christmas. Barnaby is a project for workshoppers with a *few* power tools and a penchant to get into something big like a boat. I don't need to take a poll to know how many of you guys have been confounded by construction curves, bludgeoned by blueprints, outwitted by offsets, lashed by loft lines and intimidated by terminology that was designed more to confine you to lacquering loveseats than to launch you on boat-building.

Check the bevel of the chines and keelson with
a fairing stick so that the planking will lie flush.

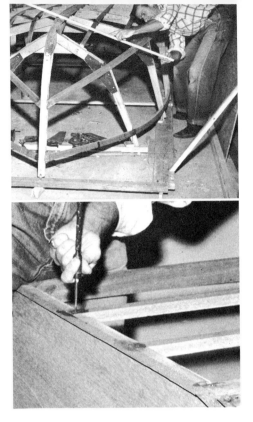

Pressure is exerted with the knee to bend the
chines in for fastening them securely.

Stringers go into notches at bottom of the transom frame, as shown. Glue and screws hold them.

PLANKING FOR THE SIDES, BOTTOM AND DECK IS CUT FROM PLYWOOD PANELS.

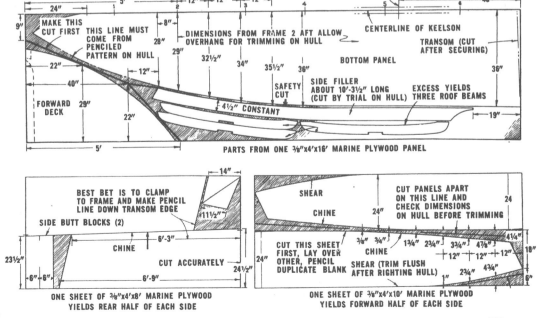

USE 16' PANEL OR BUTT 12' AND 4' PANELS HERE

MAKE THIS CUT FIRST THIS LINE MUST COME FROM PENCILED PATTERN ON HULL

DIMENSIONS FROM FRAME 2 AFT ALLOW OVERHANG FOR TRIMMING ON HULL

CENTERLINE OF KEELSON

TRANSOM (CUT AFTER SECURING)

BOTTOM PANEL

FORWARD DECK

SAFETY CUT

SIDE FILLER ABOUT 10'-3½" LONG (CUT BY TRIAL ON HULL)

EXCESS YIELDS THREE ROOF BEAMS

4½" CONSTANT

PARTS FROM ONE ⅜"x4'x16' MARINE PLYWOOD PANEL

BEST BET IS TO CLAMP TO FRAME AND MAKE PENCIL LINE DOWN TRANSOM EDGE

SIDE BUTT BLOCKS (2)

CHINE

CUT ACCURATELY

ONE SHEET OF ⅜"x4'x8' MARINE PLYWOOD YIELDS REAR HALF OF EACH SIDE

SHEAR

CHINE

CUT PANELS APART ON THIS LINE AND CHECK DIMENSIONS ON HULL BEFORE TRIMMING

CUT THIS SHEET FIRST, LAY OVER OTHER, PENCIL DUPLICATE BLANK

CHINE

SHEAR (TRIM FLUSH AFTER RIGHTING HULL)

ONE SHEET OF ⅜"x4'x10' MARINE PLYWOOD YIELDS FORWARD HALF OF EACH SIDE

But don't be afraid of this boat. It looks like work, and it is, but you will be amazed at how quickly it progresses.

My advice for starting is this. Study the six frame, or rib, drawings given here. Then order the lumber for them cut to the lengths specified and assemble them into frames with Weldwood glue, screws and bolts. When you have completed the six simple rib frames, you are looking at your actual boat coming to life.

To work from these pages, lay out the frame lines full-size on large Kraft paper. Bisect the paper with a center line. Draw each outline in a different color crayon to avoid confusion. Starting at the bottom of the sheet, lay each frame a few inches above the last. The dimensions will keep you out of trouble, plus the fact that all frames are cut on straight lines. This is a planing hull with shallow V bottom. The flat bottom makes it safe with any load and certainly makes it extremely easy to secure the bottom plywood panels. It may pound

FASTENING AT STEM AND TRANSOM. BEVELING OF CHINE AND FITTING OF SIDES.

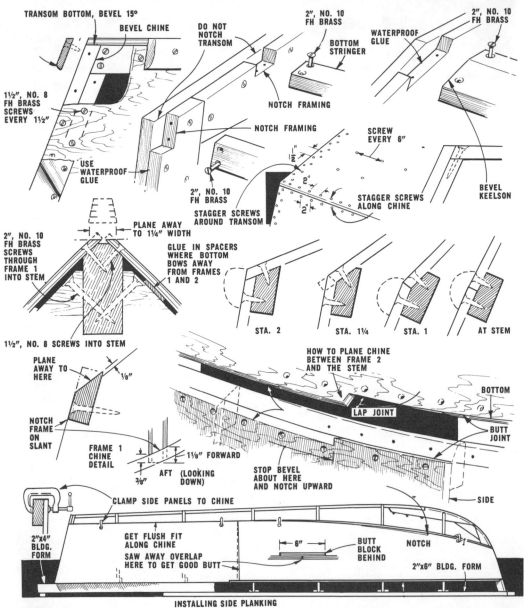

INSTALLING SIDE PLANKING

Photo here shows outlining side panel against chine and sheer of hull frame for accurate cutting.

Side panel is then clamped on to bore screw pilot holes. It's then removed for a careful gluing job.

The aft end of the bottom planking is fastened after forward end is secured in place. Crosspieces stay in until the hull is turned over, right.

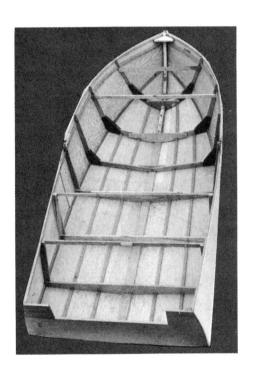

going over small chops. Adding a slight bow to each frame bottom member will soften whatever pound might annoy you.

Photos show how the plywood gussets are screwed and glued to a frame joint. Oak battens join the transom upper and lower panels and form the motor clamp board. All battens are pre-notched before gluing and screwing to the transom inner face. Do not notch the transom panel itself. See drawing.

With all frame ribs now complete, along with transom and stem, you can now cut the inner keel, or keelson. The keelson is the backbone of the upside-down hull frame, which you must now set up on the floor jig. A floor jig is not necessary if you are working on a wooden floor. But a home-built boat is always a garage project, it seems, so you need the jig shown in the drawing, as you must build the hull upside down.

While the hull is still on the jig, prepare to attach the spray rails along the chine.

The cabin roof is ⅛-inch plywood which can be bent very easily. A layer of fiberglass covers it.

These do two things. They divert spray from lapping up along the hull and they seal the open joint where the sides and bottom panels meet. These can be oak, as they bump the docks, but mahogany works so much easier and is almost as hard. Before securing the rails, sand the chine edge smooth. Use glue and screws to attach the spray rails. Foot pressure helps, as shown in photo.

At this point you can start enjoying life by knocking out the jig blocks and lifting up the bow, on props, to have a look at the inside of your new pride and joy. This is really a big moment and gives you a chance to inspect joints for later attention. When you recover from this pleasure, you can lower it again and face the last "bottom" task. That consists of brushing on two coats of Firzite, sanding these when dry, and brushing on at least two coats of a fine exterior enamel of your own color choice. White Firzite was chosen because it covers the plywood grain very well and

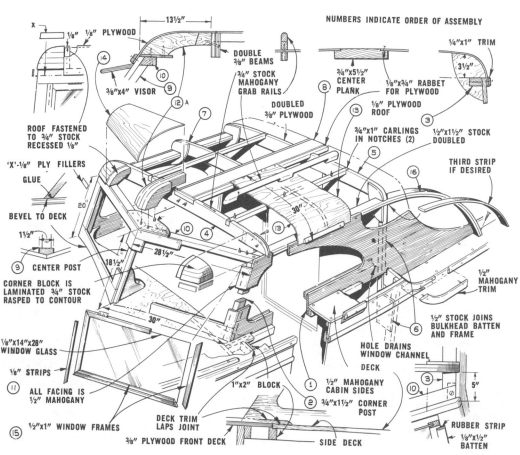

is the best base color for the white enamel that will cover the finished sides.

With the hull propped up, you can now insert the top short sheer rail and lay in the four-inch side filler panel. Reasons for this filler are worth noting. It gives you a stepped-up deck, for seaworthiness, and more room for the two bunks. Also, it gives the cabin windshield a lower profile. Best of all, it permits the use of 24-inch side panels, eliminating the need of cutting 28-inch panels out of 48-inch stock.

Before doing any "topside" work, cradle the hull securely. Oak knees joining the sheer rail to transom batten are placed only after you know the hull is resting true. Bevel ends to suit and screw through the sheer rail and through the transom batten with two-inch No. 10 screws, two per joint. Now you can put a motor on the transom. The notch was first designed to take two 15-hp motors but two mahogany wings now close it in for use with one 35-hp Bigtwin Evinrude.

Diagram across the page shows cabin construction. The circled numbers indicate sequence of building.

Sliding door is installed to save space. Opening is 18 inches wide and is framed with ¾x1½-inch stock. Door panel has cleat on the inside top which slides between a pair of cleats nailed to the roof beam. The retaining panel is being nailed in place in the photograph shown below.

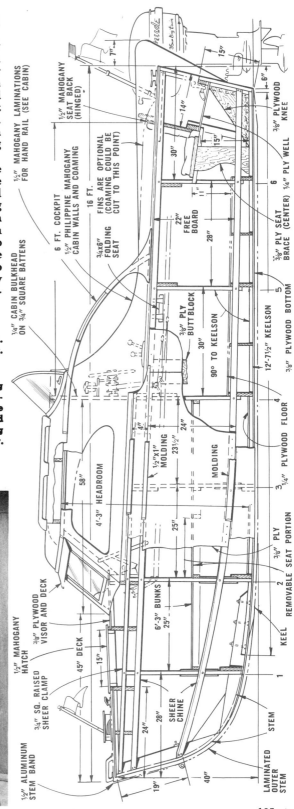

The photograph here shows a happy crew preparing for lunch in the ship's cockpit.

Diagram across the page shows exploded view of entire boat. Side planking is composed of three pieces.

Diagram below shows that the building form is made level and rigid, and the framing is erected upon it.

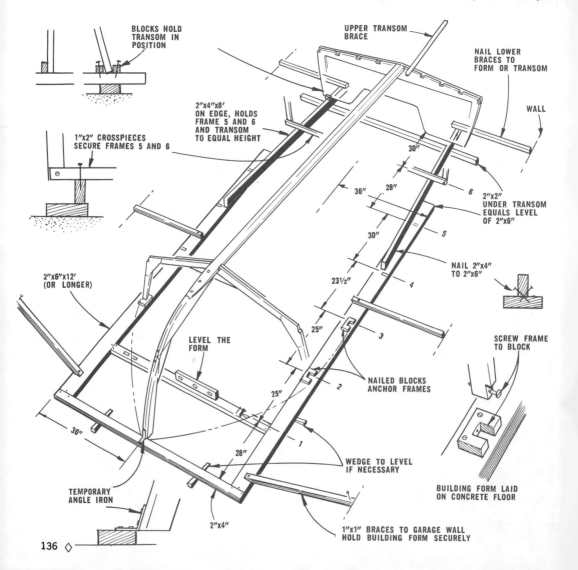

BLOCKS HOLD TRANSOM IN POSITION

UPPER TRANSOM BRACE

NAIL LOWER BRACES TO FORM OR TRANSOM

2"x4"x8' ON EDGE, HOLDS FRAME 5 AND 6 AND TRANSOM TO EQUAL HEIGHT

WALL

1"x2" CROSSPIECES SECURE FRAMES 5 AND 6

30"

36"   28"

6

2"x2" UNDER TRANSOM EQUALS LEVEL OF 2"x6"

30"

5

2"x6"x12' (OR LONGER)

23½"

4

NAIL 2"x4" TO 2"x6"

25"

3

LEVEL THE FORM

SCREW FRAME TO BLOCK

2

NAILED BLOCKS ANCHOR FRAMES

25"

1

36"

28"

WEDGE TO LEVEL IF NECESSARY

BUILDING FORM LAID ON CONCRETE FLOOR

TEMPORARY ANGLE IRON

2"x4"

1"x1" BRACES TO GARAGE WALL HOLD BUILDING FORM SECURELY

You will stand a lot on the deck, so screw and glue all joints tightly. The beam exposed to the cabin, or the "dash panel," should be mahogany. The deck is cut out of the bottom panel blank as shown in the drawing. Saw this out and repeat for the other half of the deck. Pencil the hatch opening under the deck panel and cut. Use a fairing stick to see that the deck panel will touch each beam in a smooth curve. Use half-inch Philippine mahogany for decking. This stock is duty-free and is

quite low in price. It is used extensively on this little cruiser for a big cruiser look. Four of these planks form the side decks, as in drawing.

Before starting the cabin, trim away about three inches of front deck hanging over the dash panel into a sweeping curve to where the cabin side will meet it. Cut the cabin sides out of mahogany blanks and glue the upper and lower halves together. The cockpit floor is quarter-inch plywood, cut as shown in the drawing. If you're a

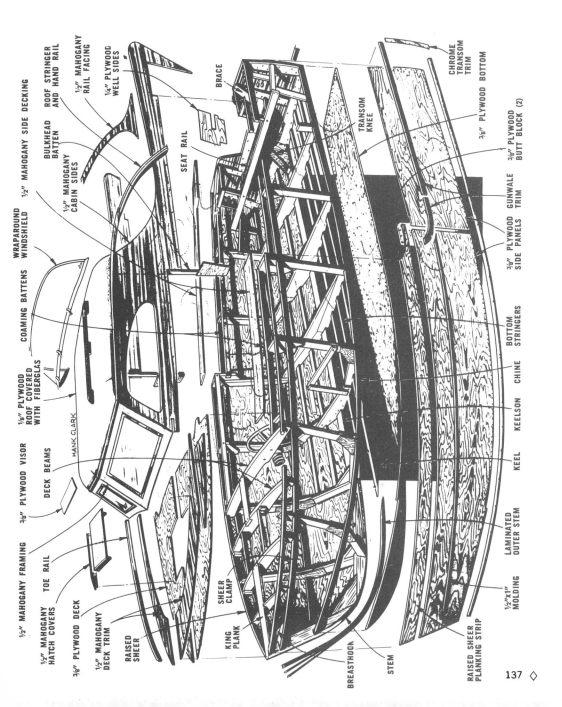

137 ◇

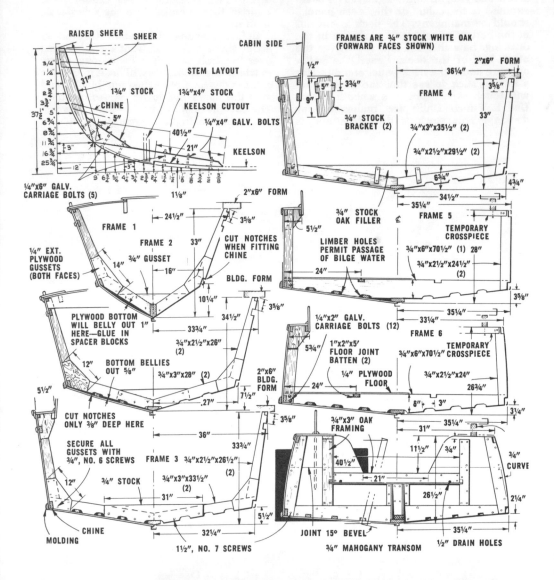

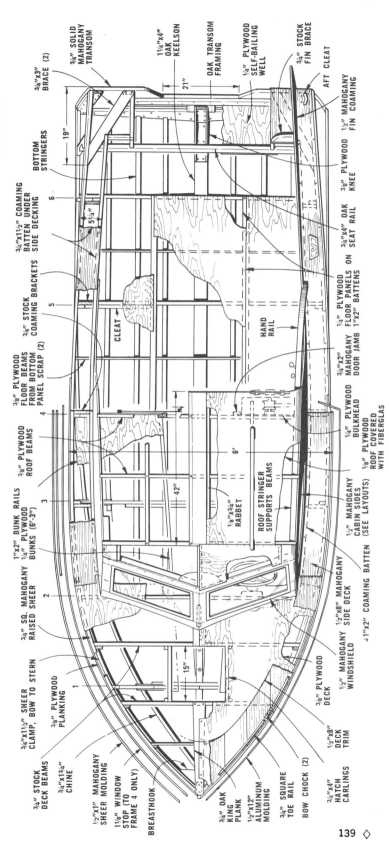

Diagram across the page gives further building details. Frames, stem and transom are built first, then erected on building form.

Diagram at the right is a plan view of hull framing. Note immediate floor beams and battens which will support the cockpit floor.

Photo below, across the page, shows the launching of the completed cruiser.

3/4" SOLID MAHOGANY TRANSOM

1 1/4"x4" OAK KEELSON

OAK TRANSOM FRAMING

1/4" PLYWOOD SELF-BAILING WELL

3/4" STOCK FIN BRACE

AFT CLEAT

1/2" MAHOGANY FIN COAMING

3/4"x3" BRACE (2)

BOTTOM STRINGERS

3/8" PLYWOOD KNEE

3/4"x4" OAK SEAT RAIL

3/4"x11 1/2" COAMING BATTEN UNDER SIDE DECKING

3/4" STOCK COAMING BRACKETS

CLEAT

HAND RAIL

1/4" PLYWOOD FLOOR PANELS ON 1"x2" BATTENS

3/4"x2" MAHOGANY DOOR JAMB

1/4" PLYWOOD BULKHEAD

3/8" PLYWOOD FLOOR BEAMS FROM BOTTOM PANEL SCRAP (2)

1/8" PLYWOOD ROOF COVERED WITH FIBERGLAS

1/2" MAHOGANY CABIN SIDES (SEE LAYOUTS)

3/8" PLYWOOD ROOF BEAMS

1/8"x3/4" RABBET

ROOF STRINGER SUPPORTS BEAMS

1"x2" BUNK RAILS

1/4" PLYWOOD BUNKS (6'-3")

3/4" SQ. MAHOGANY RAISED SHEER

1/2"x8" MAHOGANY SIDE DECK

1"x2" COAMING BATTEN

1/2" MAHOGANY WINDSHIELD

3/8" PLYWOOD DECK

3/4" STOCK DECK BEAMS

3/4"x11 1/2" SHEER CLAMP, BOW TO STERN

3/8" PLYWOOD PLANKING

3/4"x13/4" CHINE

1/2"x1" MAHOGANY SHEER MOLDING

1 1/2" WINDOW STOP (TO FRAME 4 ONLY)

BREASTHOOK

3/4" OAK KING PLANK

1/2"x12" ALUMINUM MOLDING

3/4" SQUARE TOE RAIL

BOW CHOCK (2)

3/4"x4" HATCH CARLINGS

1/2"x8" DECK TRIM

heavyweight use ⅜-inch plywood instead.

The top plate, which bends down aft to become a railing, is responsible for the straight run. The cabin cutaway drawing shows the general order of assembly. Strength is gained by doubling the roof side plate and extending it to bend down to the aft deck as a handrail. This bend also takes some muscle work. Cut all window frames and sash from scrap mahogany.

From here on the task is one of finishing. A smart move now is to use a good wood preservative. It's insurance against fungus that forms when water soaks, then dries out in the keel when you have the boat covered. Actually, this little hull is completely accessible and you can easily reach every damp spot with a sponge. Our boat is always in the yard under cover, or in the garage in really bad weather, not soaking at some berth.

Our plans for the boat this summer call for a polyethyelene cover over the cockpit with air mattresses on the floor for men folks. The gals can have the cabin. Cabin has no head but disposable units are available now. Cooking is done on a cylinder gas unit mounted on a hinged shelf in the cockpit. Nooks and corners for gear are everywhere in this short 16-footer, the real deal being the cabin.

All mahogany was spar-varnished with about six coats. Hull received three coats of white outdoor enamel. Do not paint your bottom color up along the chine to

Barnaby is easy to handle as this female skipper finds out. Boat moves easily through the water, looks like a million.

Proof of the boat's attractive appearance are these two photos. Paint boat whatever colors appeal to you. Two-tone jobs are always interesting.

Maneuverability is another feature of this boat. You'll have no trouble docking her and she's easy to climb around.

LARGE SCALE PLANS

and rib drawings are available for building boat. They are $10.00. Order from Henry Clark, 36 Highwood Drive, Dumont, New Jersey 07628. Specify Plan FB-Barnaby.

stem. This is a runabout technique. For your "cruiser" look, break it off over the chine and keep it level with water line, or a few inches above. Use masking tape. All deck hardware as well as running lights, are from the fashionable new Vollrath Viking line. We carry this baby on a Pacemaker 900 trailer, with Fulton winch, two-way ratchet. This rig has a tilt feature which helps you load or unload the boat.

All in all, Barnaby is a snappy little job that gave us loads of pleasure last year. We're all pepped up looking forward to another summer of boating. No more traffic jams, cops, flies, gasoline fumes and traffic lights. We're really starting to live—and you, too, can live it up by starting to build Barnaby. •

BILL OF MATERIALS

Size	Use	Amount
MAHOGANY		
¾"x2"x18'	Chines	2
¾"x1¼"x12'	Bottom Stringers	4
¾"x1¼"x9'	Bottom Stringers	2
¾"x18"x6'	Transom	1
¾"x10"x4'	Transom	1
¾"x1½"x18'	Normal Sheer Clamps	2
¾"x¾"x10'	Raised Sheer Clamps	2
1"x7"x6'	Cabin Dash Panel	1
½"x8"x9'	Side Decking	3
½"x8"x6'	Side Decking	2
½"x12"x8'	Cabin Walls and Fins	4
½"x12"x10'	Cabin Walls and Fins	1
½"x12"x6'	Cabin Walls and Fins	1
½"x12"x48'	Hatch Cover	1
¾"x2"x48"	Door Jambs	2
¾"x¾"x36"	Grab Rails	2
½"x12"x5'	Seat Back	1
½"x1¼"x8'	Gunwale Trim (Aft of Sta. 4)	2
½"x1"x10'	Gunwale Trim	2
½"x12'	Quarter-Round Cabin-to-Deck Molding	2
WHITE OAK		
1"x4"x6'	Rear Seat Rail	1
¾"x2½"x24'	Frame Sides	1
¾"x3"x20'	Frame Bottoms	1
¾"x6"x18'	Frame Bottoms	1
¾"x3"x9'	Transom Framing	1
1"x1¼"x18'	Keel	1
1⅛"x4"x13'	Keelson	1
2"x4"x74"	Stem	1
2"x5"x18"	Stem	1
¾"x6"x7'	Gussets (Frames 1, 2, 3)	1
EXTERIOR FIR PLYWOOD		
¼"x4'x8'	Floor, Bunks	2
⅜"x4'x16'	Bottom and Deck Planking	2
⅜"x4'x8'	Rear Sections of Side Planking	1
⅜"x4'x10'	Front Sections of Side Planking	1
¼"x30"x30"	Gussets (Frames 1, 2, 3)	1
⅛"x32"x6'-6"	Cabin Roof (Ext. Flush Door Stock)	2
SPRUCE OR FIR		
¾"x6"x4'	Center Roof Plank	1
¾"x12"x64'	Rear Seat	1
1"x2"x24'	Bunk Frames	1
1"x2"x6'	Floor Battens	2
½"x1"x12'	Side Molding	2
1"x6"x9'	Deck Beams	1
1"x3"x6'	Hatch Carlings	1

CANVASBACK

by S. Calhoun Smith

Build this kayak with hand tools and C-clamps

THIS kayak is the answer for young people who want to build an inexpensive boat for summer fun. We turned out several Canvasbacks at exactly $41.81 apiece—and each took only a week of spare time. A shop full of power tools isn't necessary, either. Ours consisted of a power jig saw and a quarter-inch electric hand drill. But all the work can be done with ordinary hand tools and a few C clamps.

Canvasback will carry one adult but it's handiest when paddled by a youngster. The boat is stable in the water and, even though it can be turned over, it won't sink. It's also light enough to be carried with ease. Building is so simple that the "jig" consists of only two blocks and a few bricks.

Apart from the exterior plywood, boat grade spruce is the best lumber to use for Canvasback. The next choice would be a good grade of fir. If you cannot obtain either of these, top-grade white pine can be purchased at most lumberyards. You can get 12-foot lengths of 1x4 or 1x6 (actual thickness about ¾ inch) and have them planed to ⅝-inch thickness and ripped into the three required widths.

Canvasback can be built on any flat surface. Begin by cutting the stem, stern and frames from exterior plywood as detailed in the drawing shown here. To simplify matters later on, you can also mark the fastening points for the stringers on each frame. Next cut the keelson to the exact length. You're then ready for the three steps shown in the construction drawings. Step 1 consists of gluing and screwing the stem and stern to the keelson, marking the frame locations and putting one-inch blocks under the stem and stern. In step

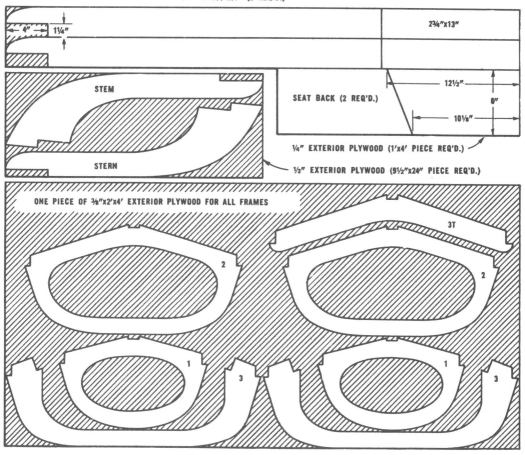

COCKPIT COAMING 2¾"x35" (2 REQ'D.)

4" 1¼"

2¾"x13"

STEM

STERN

SEAT BACK (2 REQ'D.)

12½"

10⅛"

6"

¼" EXTERIOR PLYWOOD (1'x4' PIECE REQ'D.)

½" EXTERIOR PLYWOOD (9½"x24" PIECE REQ'D.)

ONE PIECE OF ⅜"x2'x4' EXTERIOR PLYWOOD FOR ALL FRAMES

2, you add the frames, making sure they're vertical and square with the keelson. Then you nail temporary spreaders across the open tops of the two center frames. Step 3 calls for the addition of about four bricks at the center to hold the curve of the keelson. Then you add the sheer clamps which are exactly 12 feet long.

Before attempting to fasten the sheer clamps, look at the plan drawing for the measurements which give the frame locations on the sheer. Mark each sheer clamp at the center and then mark the frame locations on either side of the center mark. Next temporarily screw the sheer clamps to the No. 3 frames and bend them in so that you can mark their ends for beveling where they meet the stem and stern. Be sure the No. 1 and No. 2 frames are located properly when you do this or the sheer clamps will not curve correctly. After marking, remove the sheer clamps, cut the bevels with a saw and sand them smooth. Then install the sheer clamps permanently with glue and screws. Proceed from the center frames toward the

All edges of the completed boat frame must be planed and sanded smooth so that the canvas cover will not wear at any spots. This is important.

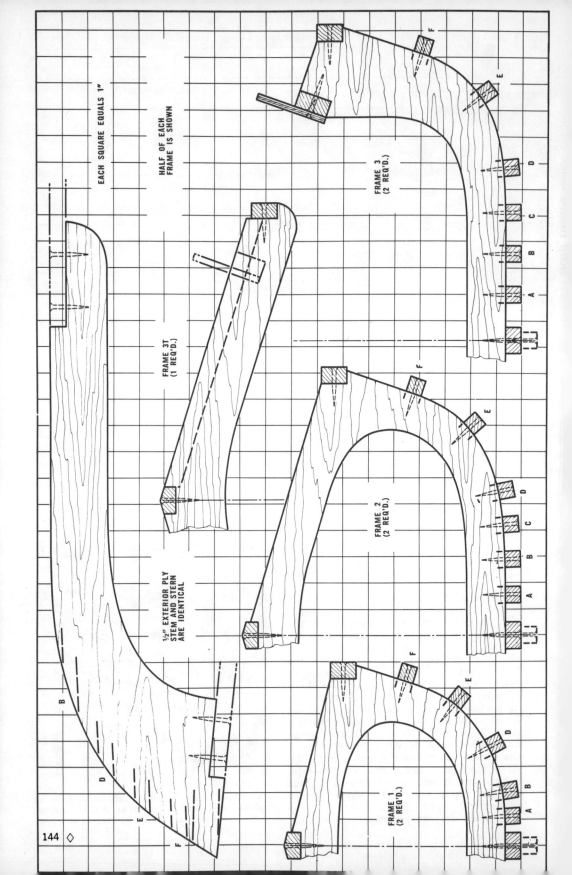

EACH SQUARE EQUALS 1"

HALF OF EACH
FRAME IS SHOWN

FRAME 3
(2 REQ'D.)

FRAME 3T
(1 REQ'D.)

FRAME 2
(2 REQ'D.)

½" EXTERIOR PLY
STEM AND STERN
ARE IDENTICAL

FRAME 1
(2 REQ'D.)

144 ◇

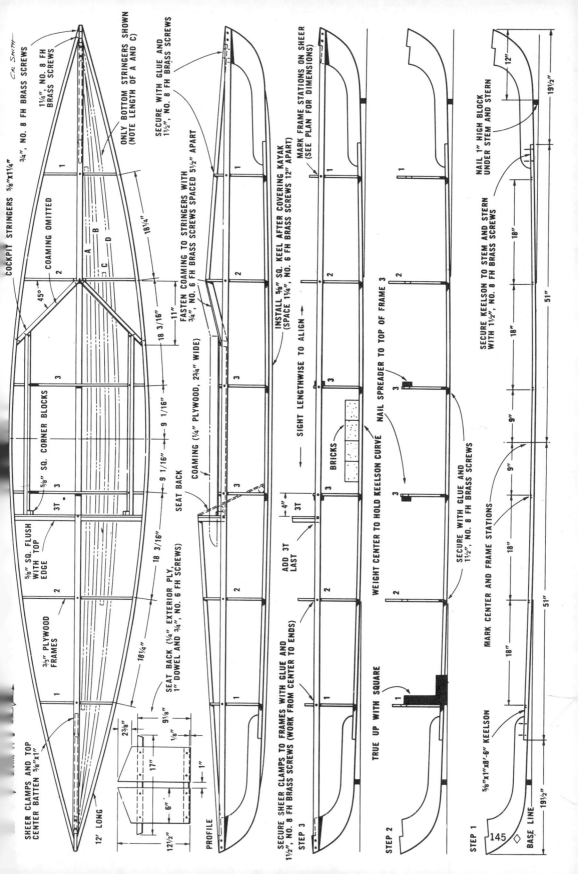

BILL OF MATERIALS

SPRUCE, FIR OR WHITE PINE

Bottom stringers and keel......13—⅝"x⅝"x12'
Sheer clamps, keelson and
   top center battens............. 4—⅝"x1"x12'
Cockpit stringers................... 1—⅝"x1¼"x8'

EXTERIOR FIR PLYWOOD

Frames .... 1—⅜"x2'x4'
Stem and stern......................... 1—½"x19"x24"
Cockpit coaming and
   seat back........................... 1—¼"x12"x48"

FLATHEAD BRASS WOOD SCREWS

Stem, stern, frames to
   keelson and sheer clamps,
   top center battens to
   frames, cockpit stringers....41—1½", No. 8
Stringers to stem and stern....20—1¼", No. 8
Stringers to stem and stern....20—¾", No. 8
Stringers to frames...............68—1½", No. 6
Keel ....12—1¼", No. 6
Cockpit coaming and
   seat back...........................24—¾", No. 6

MISCELLANEOUS

Copper tacks...........................2 boxes—7/16", No.
Waterproof glue....................3½ ounces
10-ounce canvas...................4 yards—4' width
Ambroid cement.....................large tube
Spar varnish..........................1 pint
Outside enamel.....................2 quarts
Clear dope (optional)............1 gallon

ends, fastening on alternate sides to prevent twisting of the hull frame. Drill pilot holes for the screws and clamp the plywood when boring to prevent splitting.

When the sheer clamps are fastened, deck frame No. 3T is installed. Glue and nail a ⅝-inch square strip flush with the top edge of this member before fastening it between the sheer clamps. You will note a difference between the first three photos and the plans in regard to the location of frame 3T. Originally, this member was attached directly to frame No. 3. However, it was later moved four inches aft for better back slant and body weight locations; so, follow the plans when you install it.

The top center battens go in next and then the stringers. The fastening points for the stringers are shown on the frame drawings. Attach stringer B first and then fasten its duplicate on the other side of the keelson. Then do D, E and F. This method prevents any twist in the hull frame that might occur if all the stringers were fastened on one side first. Note that stringers A and C, which go in last, do not extend the full length of the hull; all the others do. Naturally, the ends which butt against the stem and stern must be beveled and the ends of A and C should be rounded off. Sand all the sharp edges smooth so

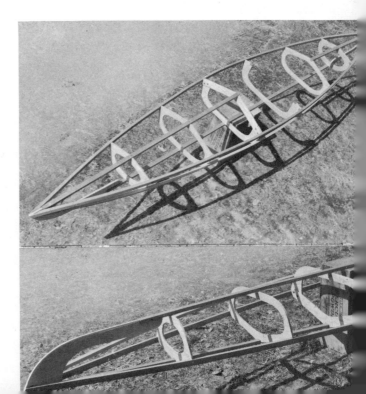

that the canvas will lie against a smooth surface. The cockpit stringers are installed last to complete the hull frame. Fit these by the cut-and-try method and then secure them with glue and screws.

The frame is now ready for covering. Take care to sand it smooth and then apply at least two coats of spar varnish, allowing each to dry thoroughly. We use 10-ounce canvas but a 12- or 14-ounce weight could be used. A four-yard length, four feet wide, is enough to cover the bottom in one piece. The decks can be covered with leftover pieces.

Attaching the canvas is a two-man operation; one pulls and the other tacks. Begin by marking a centerline lengthwise on the canvas. Start tacking at the center of the keelson, stretching the canvas and spacing the tacks about six inches apart. Work as far as the start of the stem and stern curve. Then go back to the center and stretch and tack for about a foot along one sheer clamp, spacing the tacks about three inches apart. Then go to the other side and do the same. Next add tacks in between so that the spacing is reduced to one inch. Proceed in this manner along the sheer, working toward both ends alternately. In this way, wrinkles are minimized and worked out toward the ends.

When tacking is completed along the keelson and sheer, cut the canvas along the centerline over the curve of the stem and stern. Working at the stem first, apply a liberal amount of Ambroid cement and then pull the canvas around from one side and tack it on the other. Then apply more cement, pull the canvas around from the other side and tack it so that it overlaps. Last, give the joint a coat of cement on the outside. The same procedure is used at the stern.

Excess canvas is trimmed off about ¾ inch in from the sheer clamps and used to cover the decks. Begin at the rear, tacking the straight edge of one of the rough excess triangles along the top center batten. Space the tacks two inches apart. Then pull down and tack to the outside of the sheer clamp. Next put cement along the top center and overlap with another piece of canvas, tacking every inch. Then tack it along the sheer. Finish the rear deck by tacking over frame 3T. The sides are then covered to the junction of the side and forward cockpit stringers. Then the forward deck is covered in the same manner as the rear. Apply cement at all joints and overlap the canvas before tacking. Last, trim the edges neatly, apply cement and smooth them down.

To shrink the canvas tight, it is wetted thoroughly. Further shrinking can be accomplished by applying two coats of clear dope, but this is not absolutely necessary. Three coats of outside enamel completely seal and finish the canvas. Then, after painting, the keel is installed. The cockpit coaming, which goes on last, is given two coats of spar varnish before fastening. The seat back drawing is self-explanatory.

While a double paddle can be made, we suggest buying one. Should the cover ever be torn, a canvas patch can be applied with Ambroid cement. Happy boating! •

Two people have to apply canvas, one stretching, the other tacking. Copper tacks, one inch apart, hold the canvas in place, as photo above shows.

LARGE SCALE PLANS

of the frame, stem and stern members will greatly simplify construction. For these plans send $3 to Mechanix Illustrated Plans Service, Fawcett Bldg., Greenwich, Conn. Specify Plan No. B-238, Canvasback.

FROSTFISH

By Cal Smith

For top speed thrills on ice build this 16½ footer.

IF you've never experienced the sensation of flashing over the ice at 40 mph, you're really missing a thrill. Building Frostfish will put you into this exhilarating winter sport and you can do it for $100—less if you already own a sailing paddleboard, dinghy or canoe.

Frostfish was designed to be quickly and easily built. Ordinary lumber and construction grade steel are used throughout and hardware store fittings are specified rather than more expensive marine hardware. The sail and spars are adapted from the Alcort Sailfish but lateen or Gunter canoe rigs and dinghy spars and sails of 40 to 65 square feet can be used.

Completely portable, Frostfish can be taken apart or assembled in a few minutes. The body weighs 65 lbs., the runner plank is 40 lbs. and the rig is 15 lbs.—any of which can be handled by one adult. The total 120-lb. weight is easily carried on top of a car or station wagon.

This is a fun craft, easy to sail and highly maneuverable. Carrying one adult or two youngsters, she'll do 35 to 40 mph in 20 to 25 mph winds. And she's safe. With the low lateen rig, she stays down on the ice where she belongs.

Construction is reduced to the barest essentials. The body is built of 2x4's joined in an acute isosceles triangle with plywood and 1x4 crosspieces. The runner plank is a 2x8 and the runners are built of steel angle, 2x4 fir or pine and 1x4 oak. Careful selection at the lumberyard will enable you to find good clear fir or pine. Although fancy woodworking isn't involved, a circular saw and a jig or band saw will speed up building. A drill press should be used for drilling the metal parts.

Begin with the body. The sides are at a 5° angle with the centerline, so power tools can be preset at this angle. After beveling the ends, lay the sides on sawhorses and nail a piece of scrap 1x2 across

BODY SIDES are 2x4's joined in a triangle shape with plywood and a 1x4 crosspiece.

RUNNER CHOCKS are carefully aligned and clamped for boring holes in runner.

RUNNERS are made from ⅛x1-in. steel angle, then bolted completely through ⅝-in. oak. Large scale plans show details of different types.

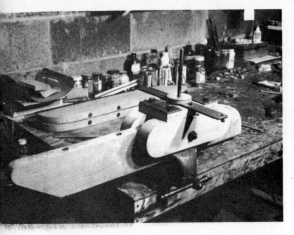

LOWERING the body of the ice boat onto the runner plank. Bolts go through angles.

STEERING RUNNER. Steel straps serve as bearing plates for bolts used in assembly.

STEPPING THE MAST. Each stay connects to eyebolt, one forward and two on runner plank.

the front end to join them temporarily. Then glue and screw the 1x4 crosspiece in place at the rear end. Next cut out the half-inch plywood crosspieces for the front section and screw the bottom ones in place. The bottom piece of the ¾-inch plywood mast step is then bored with a ¾-inch dia. hole for the steering post and fastened in place. The half-inch plywood floor is put

on later since it must be fitted to meet the runner plank cleat.

Now turn the body over and install the plywood and 1x4 crosspieces. Before screwing down the front piece, put an eyebolt in place for the forestay. Then cut the lower mast step of ¾-inch plywood to fit the foot of the mast. This piece should fit snugly inside the 2x4's behind 1x4 crosspiece and should be glued and screwed to the bottom ¾-inch plywood panel. The 2¼-inch mast step hole should be located a quarter-inch forward of the hole in the top panel to give a 3° rake to the mast. Bore the top mast step panel for the mast and steering post and screw it in place, shifting it to align the mast and post accurately.

With the crosspieces in place, the body is turned bottom up to mark the position of the runner plank. Carefully align the plank so that it will be at right angles to the centerline. The best way to do this is to measure the diagonal from the ends of the runner plank to the front of the body. The diagonal dimensions must be equal. When the plank alignment is set, attach 1x2 cleats across the bottom of the body fore and aft

of the runner plank, fitting them snugly against the runner plank edges. The half-inch plywood floor can now be screwed and glued to the bottoms of the 2x4's.

Turn the body over again to add the seat back. Bevel the edge of a 1x2 at 45° to form the seat back cleat. Screw it in place and then attach the other cleats below. This completes the woodwork on the body. Go over the whole structure with sandpaper, rounding off all edges.

The runner plank can be tackled next. If you wish to go to the extra trouble, you can make up a laminated, arched runner plank that will make the boat ride easier on rough ice. Use two layers of 1x8-in. boat grade spruce, glued while clamped in the arched position. Set up two sawhorses under each end of the plank with a scrap

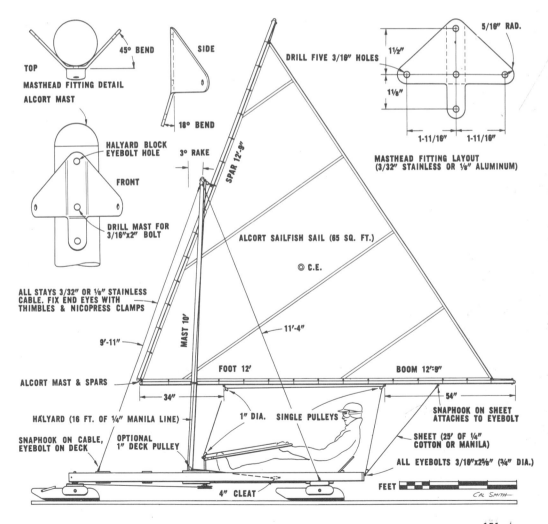

151 ◊

length of 2x4 between the ceiling and the plank center to bow down the center a half inch more than desired. Use waterproof glue and clamp the lamination at the center. Also clamp both sides every eight inches. You will need at least two dozen clamps.

The simple runner plank used on the original Frostfish is an eight-foot length of 2x8 pine. We sorted through a considerable stack of lumber to find a knot-free piece. We also selected one that was warped close to the desired arch. The plank should be carefully marked at the center and ends trimmed square. The edges are planed and sanded one quarter round except along the top edges touching the cleats under the body and on the bottom edges at the ends where the runner chocks are attached.

The runner chocks are made next. The steering runner chocks are one half inch shorter than the others. Clamp each pair together and drill for the runner pivot bolt on a drill press. Holes for $\frac{5}{16}$-in. attachment bolts should also be drilled on drill press. It is most important that the runner chocks be bolted to the runner plank

at right angles so that the runners are exactly parallel. Any toe-in or out of the main runners will only create unnecessary drag. A trick to help maintain chock alignment is to cut a $\frac{1}{8}$-inch groove the width of chock into the bottom of the runner plank so that chock is set into the runner plank. Bolt the chocks in place on the plank, putting $\frac{1}{8}$x2-inch strap bearing plates (C) on top of the plank to prevent crushing the wood when the bolts are tightened down.

The steering chock should be made next. Cut a groove for plate B in the chock tops. This plate serves as a bearing surface for the upright pivot (king) bolt. The large-scale plans contain detailed drawing of fittings such as plates B and C. Most of these fittings are cut from $\frac{1}{8}$x2-inch hot rolled steel strap. This is ordinary building construction material and should be readily available. Other metal required is also hot rolled steel of common sizes. Some hardware stores or builder's supply houses carry Redi-Rods in required sizes. One important point to remember is to give the underside of metal fittings a thick coat of paint to prevent rusting before attaching

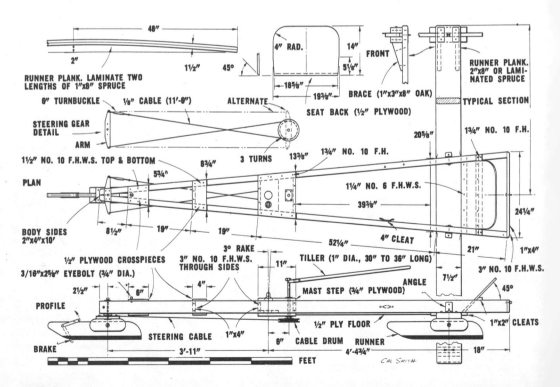

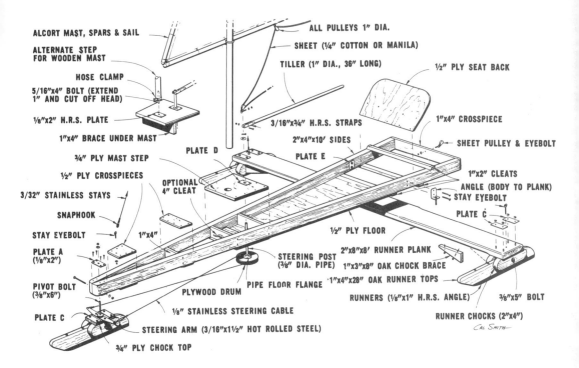

ALCORT MAST, SPARS & SAIL

ALTERNATE STEP FOR WOODEN MAST

HOSE CLAMP

5/16"x4" BOLT (EXTEND 1" AND CUT OFF HEAD)

1/8"x2" H.R.S. PLATE

1"x4" BRACE UNDER MAST

3/4" PLY MAST STEP

1/2" PLY CROSSPIECES

3/32" STAINLESS STAYS

SNAPHOOK

STAY EYEBOLT

PLATE A (1/8"x2")

PIVOT BOLT (3/8"x6")

PLATE C

1"x4"

PLYWOOD DRUM

1/8" STAINLESS STEERING CABLE

STEERING ARM (3/16"x1½" HOT ROLLED STEEL)

3/4" PLY CHOCK TOP

OPTIONAL 4" CLEAT

PLATE D

PLATE E

ALL PULLEYS 1" DIA.

SHEET (¼" COTTON OR MANILA)

TILLER (1" DIA., 36" LONG)

3/16"x¾" H.R.S. STRAPS

2"x4"x10' SIDES

STEERING POST (3/8" DIA. PIPE)

PIPE FLOOR FLANGE

½" PLY SEAT BACK

1"x4" CROSSPIECE

SHEET PULLEY & EYEBOLT

1"x2" CLEATS

ANGLE (BODY TO PLANK)

STAY EYEBOLT

PLATE C

½" PLY FLOOR

2"x8"x8' RUNNER PLANK

1"x3"x8" OAK CHOCK BRACE

1"x4"x28" OAK RUNNER TOPS

RUNNERS (1/8"x1" H.R.S. ANGLE)

3/8"x5" BOLT

RUNNER CHOCKS (2"x4")

CAL SMITH

---

them permanently in place with screws.

The runners come next. These are very important parts of any ice boat so extra care is required. Cut the oak tops to shape and sand them in smooth. Then drill for the pivot bolt on a drill press. The runners used on Frostfish consist of ⅛x1-inch hot rolled steel angle bolted flat to the bottom of the oak top. The lower edge of the angle is ground to a 45° V. This edge is also ground with a crown of about $\frac{1}{16}$ inch running fore and aft. Grinding is easier after the angle is bolted to the oak. Drill bolt holes in the angle first and use them as a guide to drill holes in the oak.

Runners should be maintained as sharp as possible by grinding and filing. The hot rolled steel will not hold an edge as long as harder steels, so when your Frostfish starts to sideslip, quit sailing and break out the file. Runners can be hardened (not tempered) or a bead of tool steel can be welded onto the running edge and ground to a V shape. This latter trick, done by a competent welder, will reduce the need for frequent sharpening.

The entire boat should be painted before attaching the fittings. Prime the wood and paint or varnish it as desired. Two or

three coats of good grade enamel should be sufficient unless the boat must be left out in the weather for long periods. Then at least four coats of enamel will be necessary.

Starting at the bow, screw the two plates (A) to the body top and bottom. Then screw on the two plates (D) for the steering post. Put the body in place on the runner plank, centering it exactly, and bolt it through the angles on the sides.

The steering gear shown gives automobile-type steering. That is, move the tiller left and the boat turns left and vice versa. You may wish to hook up the tiller boat-fashion so that moving the tiller to the left steers the boat to the right. This is the traditional arrangement and should be followed if you expect to sail against other ice boats. Simply lead the cables directly back around the drum without crossing them. If you do not wish to build a drum and cable steering gear, you can bolt a duplicate of the front steering arm to the flange on the steering post and connect the ends with auto-type tie rods. The steering cable or rods should be provided with a tightening device. Any slippage of the cable around the drum can be reduced by taking up on a turnbuckle.

Now for the go-power. We picked the lateen rig because of its simplicity and low cost. Although the Alcort Sailfish rig is not strictly an ice boat sail, it pushes Frostfish along at a good clip. It will not stand up in 40-50 mph gusts because it is not as rugged as regular ice boat sails, so exercise some caution in strong winter winds. Other sails and rigs of similar area can also be used on Frostfish. Old Town makes lateen canoe rigs of 40, 45, 55 and 65 square feet area and Grumman can supply a lateen rig of 45 square feet and a Gunter rig of 65 square feet. Dinghy sails and spars could also be adapted. Whichever rig you use, be sure to locate it correctly on the boat. Take the trouble to work out the center of effort for your particular sail as shown in the drawing in the large-scale plans. This will insure good balance and trim.

You'll like Frostfish. We've certainly enjoyed the original. There's nothing quite like zipping over the ice, and when a good gust hits you—wow! That acceleration really racks you back in the seat. If you can get your friends interested, build two or three boats and enjoy some racing. Competition adds even more zest and you'll find yourself glad to be out when a winter wind is blowing. •

FROSTFISH is quickly set up once you reach the lake, and she will give many speed thrills.

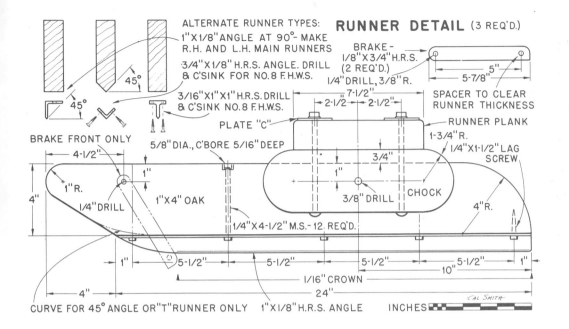

RUNNER DETAIL (3 REQ'D.)

ALTERNATE RUNNER TYPES:
1"X1/8"ANGLE AT 90°- MAKE R.H. AND L.H. MAIN RUNNERS
3/4"X1/8" H.R.S. ANGLE. DRILL & C'SINK FOR NO.8 F.H.W.S.
3/16"X1"X1" H.R.S. DRILL & C'SINK NO.8 F.H.W.S.

BRAKE- 1/8"X3/4" H.R.S. (2 REQ'D.) 1/4"DRILL, 3/8"R.

SPACER TO CLEAR RUNNER THICKNESS

PLATE "C"
RUNNER PLANK
1-3/4"R.
1/4"X1-1/2"LAG SCREW

BRAKE FRONT ONLY
5/8"DIA., C'BORE 5/16"DEEP

4-1/2"
1"R.
1"X4" OAK
1/4"DRILL
CHOCK
3/8"DRILL
4"R.

1/4"X4-1/2" M.S.- 12. REQ'D.

5-1/2" 5-1/2" 5-1/2" 5-1/2"
10"
1/16" CROWN
24"

CURVE FOR 45° ANGLE OR"T"RUNNER ONLY 1"X1/8"H.R.S. ANGLE INCHES

CAL SMITH

ADAPTING OTHER RIGS

40-65 SQ. FT. AREA

65 SQ.FT. GRUMMAN GUNTER CANOE RIG

3° RAKE→

TO LOCATE C.E., DRAW LINES FROM CORNERS TO MID-POINTS OF THEIR OPPOSITE SIDES. INTERSECTION IS THE C.E.

C.E.= CENTER OF EFFORT

LOCATE C.E. 7" AHEAD OF RUNNER PLANK CENTER.

4'-5"

CAL SMITH

POSITION MAST ACCORDINGLY

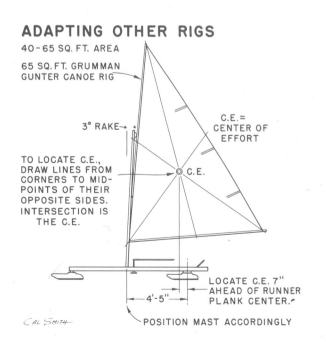

HOW TO BUILD A DOCK

Here's an easy project that'll make waterfront living more fun.

IF you're handy with a welder, you'll find it a relatively simple task to build a durable metal dock that will be the envy of your neighbors and a joy to use. If you don't weld, you can simply cut all the pieces to size and hire a welder to assemble the dock. It'll still be inexpensive.

A metal dock such as this one overcomes all the disadvantages of wooden ones: it is sturdy, lighter in weight than a wooden dock of the same strength, it's durable and can be hauled ashore during the winter months. This last point is very important

in northern areas, where high water and ice can wreck a wooden dock in no time. Another advantage of this unit is that, being mounted on wheels, it can be easily moved in or out as the depth of the lake varies during the season.

Keep construction costs down to a minimum by shopping around at a junkyard and by making reasonable substitutions of materials. The dock shown in the photographs was built for less than $35. Naturally, the length of the dock, and its height at the outer end, may be varied from

PERMANENT in appearance, the dock may be taken out of water in winter, to avoid damage.

CROSSBAR welded one foot in from the shore end of the frame is for attaching to a trailer hitch.

the plan to suit the terrain of your site.

Our 40-foot unit is made as follows. The bed pieces consist of two 20-foot lengths of angle iron on each side, each pair butt-welded at the middle. These are set with their angles to the inside so the 2x4-inch pieces for the walk will fit into them. After the bed pieces are butt-welded, they are turned over on level ground and the box frames, made of 2-inch angle iron, 12x40 inches, are welded at the outer end and the center. The center frame is placed over the butt weld.

157 ◊

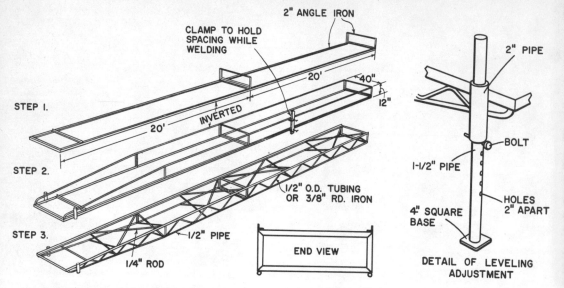

STEP I.

2" ANGLE IRON

CLAMP TO HOLD
SPACING WHILE
WELDING

20'

40"

12"

20'

INVERTED

STEP 2.

STEP 3.

1/2" O.D. TUBING
OR 3/8" RD. IRON

1/2" PIPE

1/4" ROD

END VIEW

2" PIPE

BOLT

1-1/2" PIPE

4" SQUARE
BASE

HOLES
2" APART

DETAIL OF LEVELING
ADJUSTMENT

One 40-inch piece of 2-inch angle iron is welded across the shore end, and another about a foot in from it. The latter is for attaching to a trailer hitch in order to tow the dock to its waterfront site. This completes the top surface (step 1 above).

Next comes the construction of the side framing. Half-inch pipe (about ¾-inch outside diameter) is used for the lower edge. Space it 12 inches from the angle iron, except at the shore end where it is tapered up to meet the angle iron framing. Butt weld any joints in the pipe, then weld it to the box frames at the shore end and the center. At the point where the side frame bends upward to meet the end (10 feet from the end), weld in a piece of ½-inch pipe, 12 inches long, as a spacer. You now have what is seen in step 2 of the first diagram.

Mark off the angle iron frame about every 30 inches for the zig-zag diagonal bracing and do the same on the pipe, making the markings on the pipe halfway between the marks on the angle iron. You'll have to make the markings closer together at the shore end, where the angle iron and pipe frames taper together, to maintain the constant angle of the bracing.

On the dock shown, steel tubing with ½-inch outside diameter was used for the bracing. Since an acetylene welder was used for the job, the tubing was bent and welded as the work went along. If such tubing is not available, ⅜-inch round iron will do as well. You will notice, in the photographs, that vertical braces were also used in the end section on one side; this isn't really necessary, as the frame is quite rigid without them.

About 6 inches in from the shore end, weld an 8-inch section of 2-inch pipe on

each side (see diagram No. 2 for details). These will support the pieces of 1½-inch pipe which serve as legs for leveling the shore end of the dock. Weld some diagonal cross-rods into the frame, for additional rigidity (as seen in step 3 of the first diagram), and you are ready to construct the outer end.

A front axle, wheels and tires of an old car can generally be picked up for $10 or so. After determining the necessary height of the dock at the site where you intend to use it, weld the uprights and braces between the axle and frame, and then put in diagonal cross-rods to prevent side sway (as in diagram No. 3).

If you'd like to add a rail and ladder, follow the details of diagram No. 4.

Next step is to file off any sharp edges, remove any accumulations of rust, and dress up your dock with a coat or two of aluminum paint.

The only wooden part of this project is the walk. This is made in sections that can be easily handled (as shown in diagram No. 5). Make the sections, as shown, and treat them with a commercial wood preservative for longer life. When the wood is dry, you may give the walk a few coats of aluminum paint, too. Finally, simply lay the sections of the walk down on the angle of the angle-iron frame.

At this point, you've got a dock with wheels. Now fill your old tires with a solution of calcium chloride and water, as is done with farm tractor tires. Then attach the trailer hitch, back your car up to it and haul it off to your lakeside retreat. But one final word of caution: as you're ambling down the road with this metal monster behind you, don't try any sharp turns! •

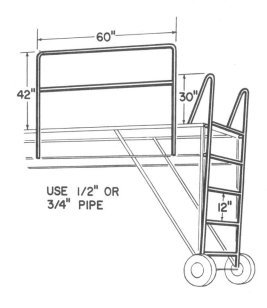

USE 1/2" OR
3/4" PIPE

60"

42"

30"

12"

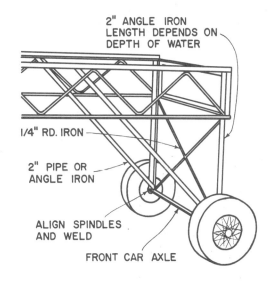

2" ANGLE IRON
LENGTH DEPENDS ON
DEPTH OF WATER

1/4" RD. IRON

2" PIPE OR
ANGLE IRON

ALIGN SPINDLES
AND WELD

FRONT CAR AXLE

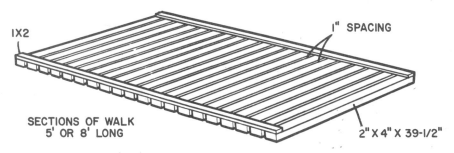

1X2

1" SPACING

SECTIONS OF WALK
5' OR 8' LONG

2" X 4" X 39-1/2"

Portable Marine Railway

IF ice and the elements in your neighbor-hood conspire to treat permanent marine railways with disrespect, thwart them by constructing this portable affair. It can be set up in the spring on any sloping beach near your camp or cottage and taken down for storage in the fall.

The winch has an 8:1 reduction and two cranks, so it will handle a boat as big as 20 feet long. It consists of a 2-in. 10-dia-metrical-pitch spur gear on a ¾-in. steel shaft and a 16-in. 10-diametrical-pitch spur gear on a 1-in. shaft. Both shafts are set in bronze bushings. The cranks go on the upper shaft and a 3-in. drum is added to the lower shaft. Fit the large gear with a pawl and install some means of locking the crank when not in use to prevent children from catching their fingers in the gears.

Use 8-foot track sections, as shown, if your beach is uneven; longer units can be employed where the slope is fairly straight. Each section consists of two 2x4-in. tracks, four 2x4-in. cross members, and two 1x4-in. rails. Spike these members together, cut half-laps in the ends of the tracks, and bore holes through the laps to take the ½-in. coupling bolts.

The first cross member on the track sec-tion farthest up on shore is made from a 2x6-in. timber. Note that it extends out beyond the sides of the section so stakes can be driven to anchor the railway. Build a 2x6-in. frame above this cross member to take the winch. After assembling the winch, bore oil holes through the frame-work and bushings.

Construct the car from 2x6-in. timbers and brace it with 1x4-in. stock. Addi-tionally brace it with two pieces of ⅛x3-in. flatbar crossed in the center and secured to the undersides of the 2x6-in. stringers. Assemble with bolts. Four 6-in. bronze-bushed wheels without flanges are re-quired. Mount them on ¾-in. steel axles and set the axles in bronze bushings in the car stringers.

The ends of the car that is detailed here are for a shallow-draft V-bottom boat. Shape them to conform with the bottom of the boat and pad with canvas or old fire hose. If your boat has a deep keel, a higher cradle will have to be constructed. For a round-bottom craft, make paper or cardboard patterns of the bottom curves, transfer the shapes to 2x12-in. stock, and band-saw the pieces to fit.

—Hi Sibley. •

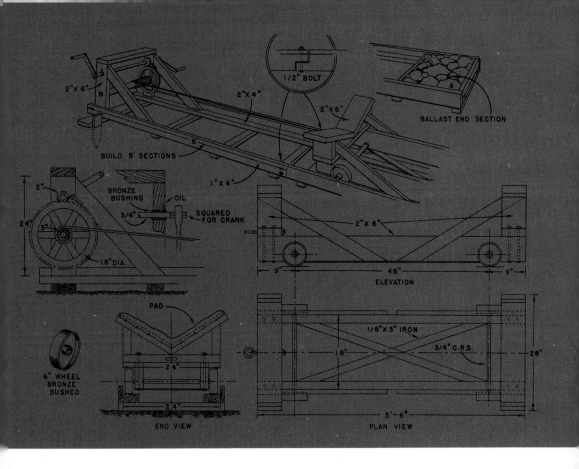

1/2" BOLT

2" x 6"

2" x 4"

2" x 6"

BALLAST END SECTION

BUILD 8' SECTIONS

8'

1" x 4"

2"

BRONZE BUSHING

OIL

3/4"

SQUARED FOR CRANK

24"

3"

16" DIA.

2" x 6"

48"

9"

9"

ELEVATION

6" WHEEL BRONZE BUSHED

PAD

2 4"

2 4"

END VIEW

1/8" X 3" IRON

3/4" C.R.S.

1 8"

2 8"

5'- 6"

PLAN VIEW

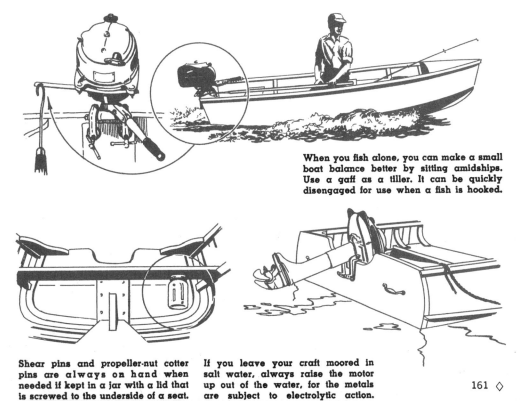

When you fish alone, you can make a small boat balance better by sitting amidships. Use a gaff as a tiller. It can be quickly disengaged for use when a fish is hooked.

Shear pins and propeller-nut cotter pins are always on hand when needed if kept in a jar with a lid that is screwed to the underside of a seat.

If you leave your craft moored in salt water, always raise the motor up out of the water, for the metals are subject to electrolytic action.

Tilting Trailer

By Joseph Adams

Save trouble and toil by building a trailer that

makes it easy to launch and haul out your boat.

FEATURING a tilting cradle and a winch, this small boat trailer can be built with tools possessed by practically every handy man. Some welding is required, but that can be done at a local shop while the bulk of the work progresses. When the job is done, the wooden frame will even outlast steel, especially around salt water.

Before starting construction, procure the front end of a small car, preferably a Crosley. Have the axle and tie rod cut, pieced out and welded so that the width between wheels is 54 inches. Have one spindle welded in position, leaving the other free for adjustment.

While the welding is being done, buy the lumber. Get a good grade of hardwood, such as fir (not spruce). The stock should be clear and straight-grained, without large knots.

Start construction with the box frame. The sides, as noted in the drawing, are six feet long and the width is determined by the location of the springs on the widened axle. The front spring shackles are fixed and each one is attached with two $\frac{5}{16}$-inch bolts so that the axle will be at the center of the frame. The rear shackles float in rubber bushings, so bore a large enough hole in each side piece to take the bushing and the bolt. The whole frame can then be assembled with two $\frac{5}{16}$-inch bolts through each joint.

The stationary yoke is the one to which the trailer hitch is attached. The other, which fits inside, is the tilting

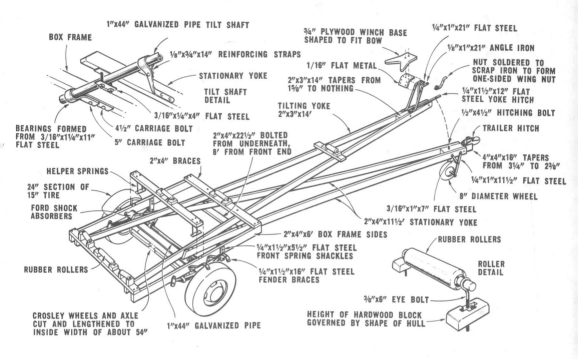

BOX FRAME

1"x44" GALVANIZED PIPE TILT SHAFT

1/8"x3/4"x14" REINFORCING STRAPS

STATIONARY YOKE

TILT SHAFT
DETAIL

3/16"x1/4"x4" FLAT STEEL

BEARINGS FORMED
FROM 3/16"x1 1/4"x11"
FLAT STEEL

4 1/2" CARRIAGE BOLT

5" CARRIAGE BOLT

2"x4" BRACES

HELPER SPRINGS

24" SECTION OF
15" TIRE

FORD SHOCK
ABSORBERS

RUBBER ROLLERS

CROSLEY WHEELS AND AXLE
CUT AND LENGTHENED TO
INSIDE WIDTH OF ABOUT 54"

1"x44" GALVANIZED PIPE

3/4" PLYWOOD WINCH BASE
SHAPED TO FIT BOW

1/16" FLAT METAL

2"x3"x14" TAPERS FROM
1 5/8" TO NOTHING

TILTING YOKE
2"x3"x14'

2"x4"x22 1/2" BOLTED
FROM UNDERNEATH,
8' FROM FRONT END

2"x4"x6' BOX FRAME SIDES

1/4"x1 1/2"x5 1/2" FLAT STEEL
FRONT SPRING SHACKLES

1/4"x1 1/2"x16" FLAT STEEL
FENDER BRACES

HEIGHT OF HARDWOOD BLOCK
GOVERNED BY SHAPE OF HULL

1/4"x1"x21" FLAT STEEL

1/8"x1"x21" ANGLE IRON

NUT SOLDERED TO
SCRAP IRON TO FORM
ONE-SIDED WING NUT

1/4"x1 1/2"x12" FLAT
STEEL YOKE HITCH

1/2"x4 1/2" HITCHING BOLT

TRAILER HITCH

4"x4"x16" TAPERS
FROM 3 1/4" TO 2 3/8"

1/4"x1"x11 1/2" FLAT STEEL

8" DIAMETER WHEEL

3/16"x1"x7" FLAT STEEL

2"x4"x11 1/2' STATIONARY YOKE

RUBBER ROLLERS

ROLLER
DETAIL

3/8"x6" EYE BOLT

yoke. To make the stationary yoke, attach two 11½-foot 2x4's to the tapered nose piece with three ⅜x7½-inch bolts, allowing four inches of the nose piece to project at the front for the trailer hitch. (Two of the bolts will later hold the front wheel assembly.) The yoke is then spread, with a crosspiece on the underside, so that the ends fall five inches inside the box frame, leaving room to mount the shock absorbers.

The stationary yoke is secured to a one-inch pipe which rotates in strap bearings attached to the undersides of the box frame seven inches in front of the axle. To keep the pipe from shifting, place a large washer on each end and secure it with a cotter pin.

The tilting yoke is made the same way as the stationary yoke except that the nose piece tapers to zero at the front end and both the nuts and heads of three $\frac{5}{16}$-inch bolts used to attach the sides are countersunk. A crosspiece,

Top of yoke is raised 14 in. above ground by a wheel of 8-in. diameter.

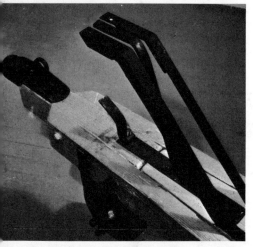

Nut with welded handle is removed when you have to raise tilting yoke.

Plywood piece, cut to bow contour, is secured between winch and mount.

Pipe to which stationary yoke is fastened turns in two bearings made of flat steel.

which bears a roller, is bolted to the top of this yoke about three feet from the end; it should be wide enough so that the ends rest on the stationary yoke. Bear in mind that the spread of the yoke should be such that there is a ⅛-inch space between the yokes when they are fitted together. (This also applies at the nose.)

The winch mount is made up of two pieces of 21-inch angle iron and one piece of flat steel. Two inches from each end, a V is cut in one side of the angle iron. The ends are then bent down at 45° angles and welded. Cut one side of the angle iron away at the lower end so that you will have a flat base. The two members are secured ten inches from the end of the tilting yoke with two $\frac{5}{16}$-inch bolts. The center piece of flat steel is bent to rise more abruptly and meet with the outside members. Beneath this center piece, another piece of flat steel is bolted; it extends to hitch the two yokes together and the forward end is secured to a bolt in the stationary yoke with a one-sided wing nut made as illustrated. The top of the mount is reinforced with a piece of flat metal and a ¾-inch piece of plywood extended in a fork to fit the bow of the boat. When the winch mount is installed, the tilting yoke can be attached to the under-sides of the box frame crosspieces with two $\frac{5}{16}$-inch bolts at each joint.

The front wheel, which is attached to the stationary yoke, is a small industrial type, eight inches in diameter. The flat steel supports are drilled to accept two of the bolts through the nose piece. When the installation is complete, the top of the yoke should be 14 inches above the ground.

Six wringer rollers are used on the box frame and tilting yoke. Five of these are

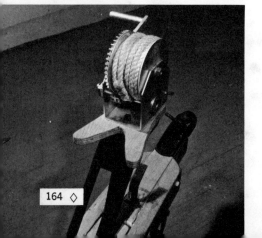

The stationary yoke is fastened to pipe with bolts and steel straps.

cut in half; the center back one is used full width. They are installed as shown in the drawing, with the outside ones tilted to fit the contour of the boat bottom.

If a Crosley front end is employed, shock absorbers from a Model A Ford will literally fall in place as illustrated. We found the Crosley springs a little light for a heavy, 16-foot runabout loaded down with a 35-hp motor and all the equipment needed for a week end camping and fishing trip. To remedy this, helper springs which bear on the axle were added. They are nothing more than heavy valve springs from a large truck motor slipped over $\frac{7}{16}$x7-inch bolts and secured with pieces of flat steel. Each assembly is attached to the center cross-piece so that the bottom is about one inch above the axle. For additional compression, light car valve springs can be inserted within the heavy springs.

Fender braces are first fashioned from light metal. Once the shape is determined, they are duplicated in the heavier steel indicated on the drawing. The heavy steel can be bent with a 20-ounce hammer in a large vise without heating or strenuous effort. Clamp the braces in position, remove the wheel and bolt them in place.

The fenders are cut from tires slightly larger than those used for the trailer. We found that 15-inch tires have just the right contour for the 12-inch Crosley wheels. Simply outline the tire section with grease and cut with a heavy pocket knife. The grease lubricates the blade. Attach each fender to the brackets with four stove bolts, using washers under the heads.

After being given a coat of paint, your trailer is finished. You'll find that it looks as good as any on the road. •

Helper springs are made of flat steel, truck valve springs and bolts.

Fender supports are shown clamped to frame for a check on shape and location.

Shock absorber from Model A Ford fits fine on the Crosley axle.

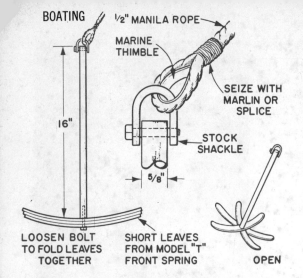

BOATING

½" MANILA ROPE

MARINE THIMBLE

SEIZE WITH MARLIN OR SPLICE

STOCK SHACKLE

16"

5/8"

LOOSEN BOLT TO FOLD LEAVES TOGETHER

SHORT LEAVES FROM MODEL "T" FRONT SPRING

OPEN

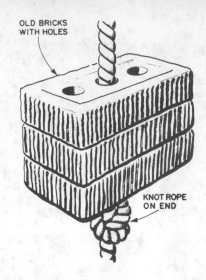

OLD BRICKS WITH HOLES

KNOT ROPE ON END

Use ⅝-in.-dia. cold rolled steel for shank and standard shackle with 11/16-in. opening for this light anchor. Drill holes for shackle and retaining bolts in lower end with latter being tapped. When loosened, spring leaves fold up for easy stowing.

A length of rope with two or three knots in one end and several discarded bricks can be made into a very satisfactory anchor. Put unknotted end of the rope through holes in the bricks, slide them down to knot, and anchor is ready to use.

BOATING TIPS

Lacking the regular wooden barrel available at boat yards for testing and cleaning outboards, use a large, clean ash can for this purpose. Remove plug from motor, then pull motor through slowly to circulate water through intake manifold, etc.

You can build and install a white stern light for your boat, as shown below. The removable staff is locked in its socket by a spring clip and pin. The dimensions below can be altered to bring the light directly over the boat's center line.

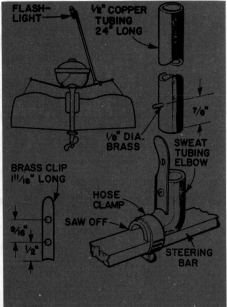

FLASH-LIGHT

½" COPPER TUBING 24" LONG

⅛" DIA. BRASS

7/8"

SWEAT TUBING ELBOW

BRASS CLIP 1¹¹/₁₆" LONG

9/16"

½"

HOSE CLAMP

SAW OFF

STEERING BAR